TRUTH, LIES AND LOVE

TRUTH, LIES AND LOVE

SANDRA BISKIND

First published in Australia in 2002 by Emissary Inc.
Level 14, Main Office Tower
Financial Park Complex
Federal Territory of Labuan
87000, Malaysia

Copyright © Emissary Inc. 2002
Copyright © in the illustrations/symbols - Emissary Inc.

National Library of Australia Cataloguing-in-Publication Entry

ISBN 983-41097-0-9

Printed in Australia by Brown Prior Anderson
Melbourne, Australia

CONDITIONS OF SALE

All rights reserved. No part of this publication may be reproduced, stored in a retrieval system, or transmitted in any form or by any means, electronic, mechanical, photocopying, recording or otherwise, without the prior permission of the publisher.

This book is sold subject to the condition that it shall not, by way of trade or otherwise, be lent, re-sold, hired out or otherwise circulated without the publisher's prior consent in any form of binding or cover other than that in which it is published and without a similar condition being imposed on the subsequent purchaser.

This book is dedicated to God and His emissaries,

especially Jo Howell and Halima McEwen.

These spiritually intelligent women illuminate my life

with love. Their guidance is precious beyond words as

we empower each other's hearts to grow in God's light.

My life is blessed by your presence.

I love you.

Acknowledgements

This book had its beginnings in my heart from early childhood. Through God's grace, Daniel Biskind was brought into my life with gifts that encouraged, complemented and completed my being.

Daniel, thank you for your amazing grasp of the English language, for your total understanding and congruence with the information in this book and the countless hours you devoted to its release.

Lynda Yanks, my beloved spiritual sister, thank you for your wisdom, prayers, insights and many editing hours.

Bill Bryant, Peter Biskind, Jo Howell, John Oliver, Lara Anderson, Ali Quedley, Buddha Boudreaux and Marie-Helene Roussell…thank you, my beloved friends and family, for your constructive and philosophical input.

Thank you Airini Kingi for your help with the computer and Al Garrotto for your editorial assistance.

I am especially grateful for the love, support and encouragement of my family and friends who have bravely participated in the intensity of my spiritual life. I know it's not always easy being around someone called to live in the light of God's truth.

CONTENTS

Acknowledgements		vi
A personal note to the reader		viii
INTRODUCTION		1
Part I	TRUTH: An Overview	13
Part II	LUCIFER'S LIES	73
Part III	LOVE: Jesus Weeps	139

A personal note to the reader

As a small child I remember often admonishing myself, "Sandra, you've got a problem, your heart is too big." At four, I told my mother I was going to be a priest. She calmly told me that would be impossible. Apparently, you had to be Catholic and a man.

The next day I told her I would be a nun. Patiently, she explained what a nun was and again pointed out I was not Catholic. As I walked away from all this bad news, I remember thinking — "Don't worry Mummy, when I grow up things will have changed. I will be a priest."

I had a mission and a purpose for being alive. My boss was just waiting for me to grow up to start work for Him.

At fourteen, standing on a wharf, waving goodbye to my grandfather on his world cruise, I knew I would never see him alive again. He died that night. At eighteen, after almost dying myself, I was given the first prophetic dreams I remember. They were about my mother's death, one every week for three weeks until the accident.

I told myself I must never love like that again and prayed that I be the next to die. In my twenties, having somewhat shut down my heart, I became immersed in the world of business.

At the age of thirty, I began sitting with spiritual masters and teachers. Once again, I consciously dedicated my life to being of service to God. Everything changed from then on.

I must have grown up enough, for God called me forth as of that moment and began to orchestrate my life.

As well as running four boutiques, I was soon writing for spiritual magazines in Australia and New Zealand, doing a morning talk on local radio, leading seminars, guest speaking for charities, consulting for businesses from this new perspective, putting on spiritual festivals and taking the course to become ordained in the Geelong Christian Spiritual Church.

Reverend Arthur Waters told me my destiny was not to be confined to a little church in Geelong and that he had a vision that saw me called to the whole world.

On a fateful Tuesday in November, 1998, I drove to Melbourne to sit with Mother Amar, an enlightened being from India. During the drive the familiar voice inside asked me, "What would you give up to know God in every breath, to be a fully enlightened being?"
"Everything!" came the spontaneous answer, out loud.

In Auckland, two weeks later to the day I met Daniel Biskind. The same voice told me that, at forty-five, I was going to marry this man and I would have to leave everyone I knew and loved, everything I had ever worked for and come and live in New Zealand.

The next time I saw Daniel, he asked me to marry him. I left for Australia the next day, only to return to Auckland three weeks later. Over dinner we agreed to be married. This was the third time we had met.

I had given God the right answer and He was taking me at my word. A new life began.

Since then I have been ordained as a priest in the Sufi Order of the West. Daniel and I created a retreat in the Bay of Islands. Purpose built on one of New Zealand's power sites, Eagles Nest is a haven for people in leadership positions to pursue spiritual development and regeneration.

Truth, Lies and Love was brewing for many years.
It is the product of twenty years of spiritual development.
Jesus has always been my constant companion.
The Ancients have been a very real presence in my life for the past six years. I knew it was only a matter of time before I would be called to share these stories with you.

Lynda, my spiritual sister, phoned weekly from America with the same message, "Every time I pray, God asks, 'Where's My book?' San, please finish the book so I can move on to other things."

In America twelve months earlier, inspired by God's urgings, I had written twenty pages. At the time, I was impressed but not particularly attracted by a story about Lucifer. Hardly my subject of choice.

Part One of the story was written in Australia. We were taking a break and wanted only sunshine and warmth but God had other plans. As the Ancient's displays of thunder and lightning lit up the sky, I constantly felt as though my head would burst with pain — an all too familiar symptom of their presence.

It was the middle of our summer but the storms in Geelong started the day we arrived and the temperature dropped well below average. In hindsight, I could have started writing in the thunder and lightning we thought we were leaving in New Zealand.

We continued searching for sunshine. The day we arrived in Brisbane the storms began. After three days of rain, we continued northward and arrived in Noosa Beach to the most awesome thunder and lightning we had ever seen.

With my head still pounding we packed up and headed off to the one place we could be assured of sunshine and warmth: Far North Queensland.

The day after we arrived, the storm clouds came rolling in. The persistence of the Ancients' phenomena had won. "Okay, God. I finally got the message." I realized that the electrically charged energy of His emissaries would be urging me to write no matter where we were.

I finally began to write as the storm raged over our house. Clear blue skies could be seen everywhere else.
I knew it was time to complete the book.

Once the decision was made, the flow began and would not stop. With joyful anticipation, I could hardly wait for the stories to unfold. Without a plan, all the years of spiritual practice and experience allowed the words to come alive inside my head with their own force.

Back in New Zealand, continuing the second part of *Truth, Lies and Love,* was a completely different experience.

By the end of Lucifer's Lies, I was longing for the pain of the Ancients rather than the disruption and heartache of this story.

Minor disasters plagued us at both work and home. Water, power, telephone and (of course) computer systems failed. Spiritual sabotage is how I would diagnose the difficulties encountered whilst describing the demise from Earth angel to human. Even relationships with family members and staff developed acute conflict, confusion and pain, dramatizing the truths within these stories.

After delivering the story about how Lucifer and the other fallen angels infiltrated the minds and hearts of our unborn babies, I was so broken-hearted it took me a week before I could start writing again.

However, this story also gave us hope.
It presents powerful confirmation that the way to happiness is through our heart. But first we must understand our lies imprison us; then the truth will set us free.

Whilst writing Jesus Weeps, peace and calm enveloped our home. The experience was extraordinary. I cried with his pain and understood when Jesus wept for us. I wept for myself and the pain of my life and the pain of all the lives of all the people who had ever been.
I knew I had to open my heart even more.

God revealed Jesus to us. In demonstrating unconditional love, Jesus shows us the tenacious heart, determined to do his Father's work — then, now and forever more.

Love is the greatest force in the universe, but without the truth, even it loses its power. The impact of the manuscript kept overwhelming us throughout the editing process. We had to keep taking breaks as the power of the message kept entraining us into a deep meditative state, sometimes putting us to sleep completely.

Truth, Lies and Love exposes our deceptions and reveals the truth so powerfully it feels like a spiritual bulldozer.

The more we read and reread *Truth, Lies and Love* the easier it became to identify and move through our fears and discover more of God's truth, propelling us further into the wisdom of the love within our hearts.

May this book do for you what it has done for us.

With love and God's blessings,

Sandra

"As the whole of nature is made by God, so the nature of each individual is made by himself. Think that the same power that moves the stars and the sap in the trees is in you. By man's limitations he, so to speak, buries the divine creative power in his mind. The soul is God, but man has a body and mind of his own."

Hazrat Inayat Khan

INTRODUCTION

INTRODUCTION

Love is powerful through its vulnerability.
However, vulnerability leaves us open to feeling pain.

To the extent we allow our minds to choose to protect the heart from pain, to that extent our hearts are inhibited from experiencing love. And to that extent love's power is diminished in our lives.

Only now are we beginning to remember our divinity.

We are divine children of God, created to fully express His being, which is the all-encompassing I AM energy pervading every particle that makes up everything we know, see and feel.

This energy is love.

We all knew this truth at one stage of our being.
We do not all know this to be the truth now.
When did we give the mind authority to dictate our thoughts? To direct our lives into creating this fear-filled world in which we now live?

INTRODUCTION

How did we come to forget how powerful our thoughts are? What happened to make us forget who we really are?

Truth, Lies and Love describes how our world came to be as it is today. These stories are about our original state within the fabric of life, the corruption from that original state and the hope and help available to us now.

Whilst we subscribe to theories such as, 'We are only our body'; 'God is judging us and there is only one life after which we go to heaven or hell'; and, 'Our most important possession is our mind', this negativity will continue to have power over us. Our hearts will remain crippled within the tiny boxes of these ideas.

The results of our crippled hearts were seen and felt as we watched the catastrophic events in the United States of America on 11 September 2001. Thousands of people lost their lives by one of the most earth-shattering acts of violence since the dropping of the atomic bomb on Hiroshima and Nagasaki.

It is time to confront the reality that we live on a planet struggling with the most extreme forces of negativity and evil.

Hatred and intolerance will plague our world until we decide to change.

Now is the time to reclaim our heritage as spiritually intelligent beings. We must diligently implement our right and fulfill our duty to know the truth, whether we like the truth or not.

INTRODUCTION

To take the right actions requires knowing the truth.
We can then change our lives for the better every day.

To change our lives, not only for ourselves but for the incredibly special children of our world and for humanity's collective future, we must restore the orientation of our hearts from fear to love.

The things our minds have loved that are incongruent with God's love and right action are the very things that keep our entire world hooked into a cycle of pain.

Without God's love, truth and compassion — without spiritual intelligence — we will forever remain imprisoned in life with only limited joy, fruitlessly searching for the cures to our diseases and the reasons behind the brutality within our world. We will continue to spend trillions of dollars on this quest, never discovering the real truth.

The body has never lost its spiritual awareness.
Pain and disease are the body's cry for the need to change. Bravely, it refuses to allow us to live in denial of the truth without pain, demanding we take stock of our thoughts and feelings.

The longer we refuse to acknowledge our true feelings, the more the body will resort to pain in order to wake us up. Unless we seek to cure the cause of the pain and not just the subsequent diseases, the symptoms will worsen until eventually our bodies die.

On the microcosmic level, pain and death are the results of our inability to face the truth about ourselves.

INTRODUCTION

Macrocosmically, our once amazing planet now experiences chronic pain and faces escalating global catastrophes as a result of humanity's denial, lies, negativity and greed.

The choices we make and the priority we have given to our physical world to the denigration and exclusion of our spiritual world is the underlying cause of our sickness and pain.

Millions suffer and perish needlessly from disease or war whilst we deny the need for change.

We must help each other to accept that we have made choices that are unacceptable for us and for those we love and to truly forgive ourselves.

We need to cease judging one another and ourselves. It is time to understand that separation and pain are the symptoms of these judgments.

How can we even pretend to know what is happening in another person's life? How can we presume to know why others do and say what they do?

We have now entered an age where it is possible, indeed imperative, for us to live once again as spiritually intelligent beings, to use our inner human technology to propel us into the future of our choice. Even the complexity of the information age cannot compare to the multi-dimensional complexity of the human being.

Truth, Lies and Love describes the process whereby we can plug the technologically advanced form of life called

INTRODUCTION

humanity back into the largest, most powerful
computer of all...God.

With this revelation comes the challenge of choice.
Will we pull the plug and remain in the dark, or will we
flick the switch and power up into the light of God's love?

There are more prophets, angelic beings and divine helpers
on this planet than ever before. They are fully engaged in
an effort to reveal the truth in a world immersed in its self-
made lies and illusions.

We still have a conscience, a part of us which knows the
truth. Our whole being — body, mind and soul — lives
through the universal God-force energy that always has
access to the real truth.

This energy is supportive and nurturing by nature.
It is unconditional love.
It is not our nature to live from any other place.

If we introspect honestly when we choose anger we realize
our behaviour is based in the mind, not the heart.
We have blamed others rather than taken responsibility for
being the creators of our lives and our painful situations.

Anger, hatred and denial are symptoms of fear. They
infallibly create needless drama in contrast to the
simplicity of accepting and living the truth.

Most of us live in total denial of our words and actions,
perpetually creating illusions sustained by lies. If even one
person hears our version of the truth and validates our

INTRODUCTION

fantasy, then in our mind we have made that fantasy into reality, no matter how little it has to do with the truth.

The world is full of masters of illusion who con themselves and believe their lies are the truth.

We choose to live from one of two places: love or fear.

Right action, honesty, justice, kindness and unity can and should be normal parts of our daily lives.

A heart and mind free of fear does not feel shame, hatred or guilt and is never controlled by anger.

When we love and respect ourselves and others we do nothing that brings us shame.

When fear grips our hearts, we are held hostage on an emotional roller coaster ride which the mind perpetuates with lies.

If we do not acknowledge fear, facing it with honesty from our hearts, then we deny the fear and feed it with more lies. Avoiding responsibility, to create the illusion we are right, we blame others. Judgment and separation are the result.

Fear has become the underlying force behind most of our decisions. We are so numb to fears such as rejection or inadequacy that it is now 'normal' to express their symptoms in both behavior and in disease.

INTRODUCTION

Our mind reacts the same way to all traumatic pain.
The modern messianic mind thinks it has to make decisions for us to save us from ever feeling that pain again.

The problem, however, is that it has never been the mind's job to make our most crucial decisions. That has always been the role of the heart. Microcosmically speaking, the mind is the notebook computer, the heart is the operator and the soul is the programmer.
(God is the inventor, designer and manufacturer of it all.)

Spontaneity and joy are lost when the very thing the mind is trying to avoid at all costs — pain — is the very thing that manifests when we live within the structure of our deadly games.

There is a powerful universal order to all life.
What we focus upon we manifest in our lives.
Living under the dictatorship of the mind ignores and distorts vital aspects of this.

Humans are powerful beyond belief.
We have forgotten that we can bring our experiences into being by our thoughts.

Thoughts motivated by love beget love.
Thoughts motivated by fear beget fear.

For instance, motivated by fear of poverty we can work hard to accrue wealth. Yet, no matter how wealthy we become, the fear will remain, perhaps changing its face to fear of loss, until the underlying cause has been addressed.

INTRODUCTION

Fear-motivated wealth accumulation will only perpetuate a world system based on greed, lies, hostility and abuse, competition and corruption instead of cooperation.

Free will means we are free to choose to think what we will. That means we are free to command our thoughts rather than have our thoughts control us.

Our choice is now clear.
Individually and collectively, we can no longer afford to avoid this choice.

We can continue down the path directed by the mind, believing in separation, scarcity and duality, living the lives we have always lived, denying our spirituality and the brotherhood of mankind. This path is bringing about the destruction of our entire world. Or, we can choose the path that originates from the heart.

This path unites us through love and compassion, illuminating our lives with peace, joy, truth and wholeness.

God is ready, willing and more than able to comfort and support us, to encourage us, to awaken our hearts and to rejoice in our homecoming.

Truth, Lies and Love will inspire your heart to bravely demand the truth, challenge your mind to accept and integrate the truth and rekindle the joy of hope in your soul.

"He who fights his nature for his ideal is a saint, he who subjects his ideal to his realization of truth is the master."

Hazrat Inayat Khan

TRUTH: An Overview

TRUTH: An Overview

There was no beginning, as there is no end.
The fabric of all life has always been.

That fabric looks different with every glance because God's every in-breath and out-breath changes the landscape and all the beings of His creation.

So too, in your own personal life, the landscape — the lives of everyone and everything — changes with every breath you take.

The fabric was a loosely woven tapestry of God's thoughts. To describe this fabric in human terms you might say it was the blissful existence of pure love, interwoven with pure joy, oscillating light and sound, radiating from the heart of God.

The barriers of language did not exist. The fabric of life knew every thread as a part of the oneness of itself. The joy of the movement of light and sound created ever-changing patterns of life upon the fabric.

God, who is the fabric, reveled in this joy by continually creating new patterns across His landscape.
Every color was applied, from its lightest hue to its deepest, from a flat wash to its most luminescent.

Each color was blessed by its own sound, and every sound had its own unique color. One did not come without the other nor did one come before or after the other.

The fabric of all life was the original first dimension.
As God continued to evolve His interwoven threads of color and sound, the tapestry of His love and joy took on texture.

The texture emerged from the very centre of the fabric, from the centre of God's heart. Using the limited medium of the spoken word, this texture was born and still manifests with the force and excitement of cracking thunder and great spurts of electromagnetic energy that you call lightning.

The evolving fabric reorganized itself into yet another dimension, expanding itself within itself.

At this point in the story, it is important to understand how dualistic thought processes could easily mistake the creation or appearance of texture as something separate from the original fabric.

Just as you are one within the now tightly interwoven threads of God's existence, so too the formation of God's second dimension was nonetheless part of the same original fabric.

TRUTH: An Overview

Even though this was the first expansion into a different, more complex form of life within the fabric, this electrically charged formation of energy was still a part of the very heart of God.

This new dimension has become known as the Ancients.

They have taken on this name to be identified in this world as the first energy from God's original form.

Their texture and form was generated from the original fabric's color and sound but came into being with a radically different energetic force.

The energy within the first dimension of color and sound vibrated within a range that was much slower and more limited than this new texture.

The Ancients oscillated far beyond the original speed and range of color and sound.
They were charged with more electrons.
This formed water, magnetism and electricity.
Color and sound were intensified within the texture, too.

The worlds as you know them evolved from this first expansion of the fabric. For God so loved the dimensional changes in the fabric of His being that he continued to create new levels of existence within the one fabric.

The threads of the fabric began to not only interweave on the original level but also interwove themselves into multiple frequencies at the same time.

The grid, a complex yet straight-forward and workable information system, evolved at the same time. The grid was essential to the unity of all life throughout creation as it was the means by which all life communicated and traveled throughout the fabric, throughout the universes.

This meant the fabric itself evolved into a multi-dimensional layering within itself of color, sound, and texture. There was an order to the systems and dimensions which were all connected by God's infinite and unconditional love. Complexity, which first expanded arithmetically, then geometrically, now exploded infinitely.

This has been called by our physicists, the 'Big Bang'. Thus were the planets and galaxies and heavenly bodies formed within God's heart.

Their intelligence was drawn from the mind of God. This is not to be confused with how the mind of man works at present. It is how the mind of man was created and how the human mind worked in the beginning — completely integrated with God's love and wisdom within the multi-dimensionality of His creation.

The angelic beings were brought forth from this textural explosion of God's form and added yet another dimension and frequency to the patterns of the fabric.

They were different in every way from the Ancients. God was exploring different levels and qualities of consciousness, adding to His fabric more and more intricate patterns and dimensions of His being.

TRUTH: An Overview

The angelic beings were not as heavily charged with the immense seminal power of the Ancients. Rather, they were more ethereal and softer in nature. They were created to work in conjunction with the Ancients.

All of the threads of life reacted in different ways to God's consciously evolving energy. The excitement and joy from this evolution was shared by the Ancients and His angels. The angels began to co-create worlds with God and the Ancients.

The world in which you live, called World Earth, was their first co-creation and added another explosion of life into the evolving tapestry.
This added the third dimension.

Angelic beings who had experienced life only through pure, etheric energy were able to densify and contract life force into living bodies as we know them today.

Another glorious pattern emerged in the fabric.

The bliss of the continuing emergence and evolution of God's love coursed through the fabric and every dimension interwoven within the fabric felt and knew every other dimension through the interconnectedness of the grid.

All life existed as integral parts in the wholeness of the fabric as a drop of water exists as a part of the ocean.
And just as water exists on many levels — from its densest form as ice, then reacting with the sun's energy to become running water, then becoming vapor and evaporating into the air — so too is each aspect still a part of the original life form called water.

Thus the fabric's dimensions appeared to be separate from each other but were in fact, just like the water, the same thread experiencing life through different forms of awareness.

The Ancients and angels loved the exploration of the dimensions. Their loving creativity expressed itself in the creation of all manner of life on World Earth.

The fabric grew and grew as each new conscious soul added yet another thread and enhanced the intricate patterns of the increasingly tightly woven tapestry.

Within each dimension, every expansion developed in perfect harmony with God's order and each aspect of the fabric expanded itself as an expression of God's love.

The inventiveness of the angels and the Ancients on World Earth was without comparison. Every imaginable color, sound, shape and texture was brought into being.

The spirit of God ran freely through the heart and mind of every angel and the entirety of the energy of the Ancients. Inspired by the pure bliss and joy of life itself, they continued to experiment, creating every kind of life form — animal, vegetable and mineral.

Ultimately the angels co-created human beings, who were then known as Earth angels.

They loved color and sound, texture and form and there was no end to their imagination. Of course, their imaginations were from that infinite well-spring of wisdom that is God's love.

TRUTH: An Overview

The Ancients were the original energy to take on dimensional form within the fabric. As such, they were the most potent manifestation of God's love and wisdom.

The atmosphere crackled with their intensity, their power, and their consciousness.

Whilst the patterns and dimensions continued to further evolve, God entrusted the Ancients with the responsibility of caring for the fabric's ever-expanding energies.

This was a joy unto itself. As joy compounded, even more ways of expressing joy were created. Yet another dimension, the fourth, emerged to enhance their already ecstatic existence. This was the dimension of pure spirit.

Ecstatic, that is, until one of the angelic realm tried to control the fabric and the emerging patterns without the influence of God's love.

This angel's name was Lucifer, meaning 'bearer of light'.

Lucifer was the most dazzling of all God's angels.
If you had seen him before he began his assault on World Earth his perfection and beauty would have taken your breath away.

The light of God's love shone brightly through his waist-length golden hair, his emerald eyes, high cheek bones and strong, square jaw. His wings glittered with gold as though sprinkled with fairy dust. His being emanated light as the facets of a diamond in full sunlight.

God loved Lucifer. Like a loving parent, He deeply wanted to see him reconnect back into the original fabric.
However, Lucifer had already terminated his heart connection with God as part of his experimentation within creation.

God's commitment to free will is so great that He refrains from using force.

He wants Lucifer to come home of his own volition.

God assigned the Ancients the task of taking Lucifer and the other rebellious angels to a place that would help them make the journey back into their hearts.
The name of that special place was World Earth.

God's love permeated the atmosphere on World Earth.
The Earth angels knew that every breath they took was God breathing through them.

They knew they saw through the eyes of God and listened through the ears of God. Their hearts beat with the pulse of God's heart beating and they existed simultaneously in all the dimensions. They knew and felt their connection with every pattern within God's fabric.

The Earth angels, like the Earth's water, were able to exist in solid third dimensional human form, the fluid form of the second dimension and as the pure energy of the first and fourth dimensions all at the same time.

Life's expression on World Earth was unique in all the fabric. Its luminosity and complexity was extraordinary.

TRUTH: An Overview

Where better for Lucifer to once again feel the connection to God's love, to enable him to create from that place of wisdom?

But Lucifer did not disclose that he had made up his mind to sever his connection to God's love regardless of the outcome on World Earth.

Deviously, he hid his desires and ambition from his fellow angels and even the Ancients. Upon arrival on World Earth he was most pleased at his cleverness.

He realized he had been given the perfect opportunity to play out his fantasies in the actual heart of God. He was determined not to let any of his brothers or sisters or the Ancients stop him.

The Ancients had not been on World Earth since its beginnings within the fabric. They were awe-struck by this magnificent expression of God's love.

They empathized with Lucifer's apparently instant and complete conversion from his previous way of thinking and accepted his change of heart at face value.

God's love was overwhelming them and all of their senses and it seemed Lucifer was experiencing the same thing.

What they did not understand, as it was outside their frame of reference to know or even imagine such a thing was possible, was that Lucifer's mind was indeed reeling, but not with the knowledge or feelings from God's manifest presence alone. He intended to have World Earth as his own.

He was intoxicated by his vision of all the life upon it knowing him as its creator. The unlimited possibilities that existed on World Earth sent Lucifer into a state of rapture that the Ancients mistook for his total transformation.

The Ancients assumed his connection to God's love was once again strong and complete.
They left Lucifer and his companions to stay in this state of bliss for as long as they wished.

Most, but not all of Lucifer's angels remained on World Earth with him. He was right not to trust them with his plans, as many were overcome by the love of God and wished nothing more than to turn away from Lucifer's ideas and return to their home. They, however, were happy Lucifer had come to his senses and no longer wished to create without God's love.

The Ancients resumed their supervision of the complexity of life within the fabric and all was well, or so they thought.
It was only an out-breath in time before the plight of World Earth became known to the Ancients.

TRUTH: An Overview

After the Ancients' departure from World Earth, Lucifer explained his plan to his remaining fellow angels and assigned them into two groups. He was careful to pre-empt any opportunity for factions to start up against him and worked in close conjunction with both groups.

In the terms of our current concept of time, it took millions of years for Lucifer and the others to make the changes he wanted to World Earth and its inhabitants.

Lucifer wiped out many different phases of life during his experimentations.

His first priority was to veil the heart to God's love and rid the planet of all existing Earth angels. He knew that, in their original state of awareness, they would never see him as God.

To serve his purpose, Lucifer devised a clever plan to short-circuit the Earth angels' multi-dimensional ability to travel the fabric. He created force fields around the planet that interrupted the grid that carries all information and energetic forms to and from other dimensions.

The Earth angels could no longer reappear in human form once they had left World Earth's atmosphere. Those who traversed the dimensions, leaving their earthly bodies behind, found they could not re-enter them. Without being able to replenish their beloved bodies with their spiritual life force, their bodies died.

The destruction of the grid gave Lucifer the opportunity to wipe out all opposition. His next step was to spread a new kind of energy onto World Earth.

This energy was Lucifer's incredibly powerful brainchild. With the grid down, he deluded life on World Earth that God had withdrawn His love.

That delusion, coupled with the disruption of the grid, gave Lucifer the perfect opportunity to unveil his brainchild: fear. Lucifer nurtured and loved his seeds of fear.
These seeds sprouted, grew and bloomed in the hearts and minds of all life on World Earth.

Not until Lucifer maliciously vandalized the grid, which acted like a conduit for all information from one dimension to another, had a part of the fabric felt cut off from itself.

The fabric twisted onto itself. Distortions in the first and third dimensional layers alerted the Ancients to Lucifer's efforts to create without love.

Lucifer's disruptions threatened the very existence of the fabric. But he refused to consider the possibility that this form of creation would result in destruction and aberrations within the fabric.

In truth, he did not care. Lucifer had discovered the universal law of free will. He had no intention of reforming. He liked the idea of creating without love or light.

What he wanted was to deny the existence of love and create a dimension unique to himself. Lucifer intended to use God's love against Him, making himself the god of his own dimension — World Earth.

TRUTH: An Overview

The Ancients came back to World Earth to investigate this tear in the existence of the fabric.

By then however, Lucifer had ample opportunity to build his defense against the day when God's emissaries would want to repair and reclaim the damaged planet.

The love of the Ancients could not penetrate the barriers of fear, negativity and hatred that had grown up in and around the whole of World Earth.

God directed the Ancients to create a plan. They organized twelve entities from their own essence to implement the plan to re-establish love as the pre-eminent life force there once again.

From that moment on, the Ancients focused their energy. They explored every possible avenue for healing the grid. Without that, the consciousness of World Earth would never be able to receive the information necessary for her people to choose another way.

To their dismay, they discovered the disjointed cycle of life that had established itself and become the norm. Because the Ancients' immense power would have been overwhelming, even deadly, to those exposed to them at that time, they recruited volunteers to go to the planet to participate via the process of reincarnation.

The first to offer assistance were the angels who had been with Lucifer's original group, one of these being the Archangel Michael.

Michael's dark hair and vivid blue eyes were a part of a beauty that was rivaled only by that of Lucifer.
His wings were silver and reflected the deep purple aura around him like a brightly burning flame.

Michael carried the sword of truth within his heart, even more so since his first visit to World Earth.
His very presence burned away negativity and, just like fire, replenished the heart with fertile soil for God's seed of love to sprout once more.

These angels entered World Earth through the birth process but became heartsick as they experienced the corruption of all life there. The absence of love and wisdom in the world devastated the angels, as did humanity's ignorance of who humans really were.

With broken hearts many of these angels died quickly, unable to face the darkness of a world without love.

Many, like Michael, resolved to carry on.
With guidance from the Ancients, these noble ones persisted in their mission, which required them to be caught up in the decay of life without God.

The repairs to the grid commenced.
With every section completed, another avenue to relay information to and from World Earth was opened to the Ancients and angels.

Through the partially repaired sections of the grid, they recruited volunteers from the various kingdoms within the fabric. Many of the fairy kingdom (which is part of the heavenly realm) and the Earth spirits, known as devas, were of great help repairing this information system from within World Earth's boundaries.

Everything to do with the reclamation of World Earth was fraught with a myriad of untold dangers. These threats did not come from Lucifer and his cohorts alone. By this time, the people had been without contact from the other dimensions for so long that they feared and rejected all extra-dimensional help.

In their ignorance, not only did the people of World Earth have deep fear of the rest of all life, but Lucifer's brilliant contingency plan had been put into force. Once he realized he could not stop the Ancients from repairing the information grid, Lucifer deceived humanity en masse.

He convinced earthlings that anything they heard from within — that they felt came from their hearts — was untrustworthy, even evil. He taught them never to meditate, for this would take them into the centre of their being, into their hearts, where fear and evil reside. They were brought up not to listen to anything that came from anywhere but their minds.

He also taught them that angels, fairies and devas were figments of their imaginations and the stuff of children's fairy tales. Only perceptions of the five physical senses could be considered valid.

They knew fear so well they could never have guessed it bloomed and spread because Lucifer had terrorized their crippled hearts into surrender.

TRUTH, LIES AND LOVE

Lucifer influenced life on World Earth by terrifying the heart with fear. Such pain was new; no one had ever before experienced the horrors of a heart and mind full of fear.

Soon the heart, in full retreat, allowed itself to be cut off from its world of pain. The mind and its tools of choice, logic and reason, began to control each being. Without the wisdom of the heart, more pain was the inevitable result.

A vicious cycle began, from which there seemed to be no escape. The more they feared something, the more they drew that fear and the objects of that fear — the very situations and people they feared — into their lives.

Lucifer fed them a constant diet of lies which strengthened his suffocating death grip on their hearts.
The people on World Earth had become Lucifer's.

They rejected and even killed many of the first beings who worked to help them turn back into the fabric of life. These souls were the healers of their time, born with their hearts open to God and love's wisdom intact.

Many of these people were labeled witches or wizards because they remembered the vibration of love that had the power to heal. At first, the people wanted to be healed and held them in great respect.

It is easy to understand why Lucifer desired to be rid of these healers. They were exposing the populace to the workings of God's love in action.

This was the last thing Lucifer would allow to continue.

TRUTH: An Overview

After all he had accomplished, he would not abandon his plan without a fight.

The arrival of these children who displayed the wisdom and wonder of God's heart alerted him to the fact that his plans had been uncovered. It did not take him long to deduce heavenly powers were in fact breaking down his barriers and beginning to repair the grid.

This meant war.
Lucifer gathered his teams together. They all realized the urgency to escalate their efforts and the need to outwit their opposition.

They did not change their basic tactics. They continued to persecute and sow fear into the hearts of any souls who displayed love, compassion, selflessness or knowledge of what the people on World Earth called miracles.

Of course, by now you realize these 'feats of magic' or phenomena were not miracles at all. They were simply the way the fabric of life operated. They were manifestations of the timeless principles of God's universal order in action and the way all of life interacted in its original, uncorrupted form.

The most effective means for Lucifer's teams to undermine the angels' first attempts to reclaim the souls of their brothers and sisters was to bring the religious institutions under their influence.

By spreading lies about these gifted people who helped the rest of the community, Lucifer's potent seeds of fear multiplied and grew in the fertile minds of the men who controlled the religious establishments.

He had long since separated women out of positions of authority in most religions.

Separation of any kind is a breeding ground for conflict, domination, suppression and duplicity — the foundation of Lucifer's playground.

He targeted women healers first, for many religious men had already assimilated the lies of how woman was the source of 'original sin'. (With pride, he considered this to be one of his most successful ideas.) Closing down man's heart to the real God, to love, effectively destroyed man's love for woman as his natural other half.

After that, all that remained was the body and mind being fed more and more lustful and corrupt ideas.
To know where that took the people of World Earth, one need only survey the planet with an objective mind.

There has been no end to the inhuman inventiveness to rationalize and implement the suppression and manipulation of women.

Lucifer spread lies that almost everyone believed, making it ineffectual, not to mention horrific, for these women to continue to enter World Earth with love in this way. Many of these women, forerunners of God's army of angels, were branded witches and burned at the stake.

TRUTH: An Overview

These 'lies' were simply the truth about himself and his ways.

This was his ultimate depraved joke on humanity.
Everything he spread about God's emissaries was in fact the truth about what he and his minions were doing.

By and large most people chose to accept and believe these Luciferic lies, even when a spark of truth touched their hearts.

The fabric in all its dimensions had to be reconstituted and brought back into harmony. The Ancients and the angels had to prepare to wage war for the healing of the heart.

By the time of the Great Inquisition, this war had escalated to the point where the hope of victory required enormous faith, even for angels. Nonetheless, they were determined to help people realize they had made choices based on false information.

They were committed to reawakening the hearts of humanity, but the hearts of the people of World Earth had given up under the tyranny of fear.

The angels had suffered a great deal and needed the Ancients to participate more fully in this war.
Lucifer and his lot proved more cunning, devious and resourceful than anyone could have thought possible.

The Ancients conferred amongst themselves, taking everything into consideration. Obviously, they had the capacity to go to World Earth and annihilate Lucifer and his team.

But that is not the way of God.

God, the very fabric of life, is constructive.
Annihilation is destructive and it is against God's law to eliminate life. God's principle is to intercede only when asked. He does not intervene randomly, nor does He discriminate. His universal laws are inviolable, and He observes them, too.

TRUTH: An Overview

Consistent with God's principle of free will, the Ancients were also convinced the people had to regain their ability to reclaim their right to know the truth through exercising their right of choice.

The truth could best be perceived by exposing the lies in the light of the truth.

The Ancients realized they had to be the manifestation of God's law in action. The people had to learn to trust in them first before they would be capable of trusting in themselves once more.

Because the world had been separated into many areas, the Ancients decided to increase the number of powerful beings sent to Earth. They saw a pattern emerging through this separation and responded by focusing their attention on the two broadest cultural streams, the East and the West.

Their plan envisaged a few of them at a time in different parts of the world. They would be in human form and be born and live as normal people until they began their work to inspire humanity and remind them of who they really are. Every universal truth they expressed and embodied had to be relevant to the culture of the time and place.

The grid repairs were incomplete when the Ancients first implemented this plan. Those entering World Earth would not be able to rejoin the multi-dimensionality of the fabric whilst in human form.

They knew the dominant consciousness on the planet had permeated the entirety of every level of existence on World

Earth. Every person was affected by the belief system that Lucifer had manipulated into place.

The Ancients understood the pitfalls of losing their ability to manifest in any form at any time, but they had not appreciated how powerful the blockages around the heart had become.

The struggle to keep their own hearts from descending into fear, which would destroy their plan, quickly became their greatest concern.

Sananda was the first representative of the Ancients to go to World Earth in human body. His physical form radiated God's love. The clarity of his soul could be seen through his changeable blue-grey eyes and luminous skin. His pale brown hair flecked with gold was like a crown above the strong features of his beautiful face.

His name carried a powerful vibration of love — of God — within it. This in itself was like a magnet to the people and, of course, to Lucifer as well.

Sananda's assignment was to carry on the work of the original angels. He came to World Earth accompanied by the Archangel Michael and the other angels who had escorted Lucifer millions of years before.

These angels had learnt much about Lucifer's deceptions. They no longer went into shock when dealing with the people's astonishingly contorted beliefs.

Although humankind could not imagine how life could be

TRUTH: An Overview

any other way, nevertheless some listened to the voices coming from within their hearts.

Over many thousands of years, positive inroads into the heart were accomplished and connections made. But, even the bravest souls had been hit hard by Lucifer's takeover.

When the heart was penetrated and reignited with God's love, only then was there a chance to alter the core belief systems and resultant choices of the altered mind.

The repairs on the grid progressed to the point where finally these powerful information and subtle energy transmission lines could be used to effect increasing numbers of peoples' hearts as they chose to listen to the Ancients' words.

More and more, people turned to love as an alternative to hatred, fear and confusion. Their growing numbers posed a threat to Lucifer, who set out to understand how the people's minds were being turned from the head to the heart. In reaction, he initiated yet another powerful assault.

He convinced people in the churches and temples that listening to the voices coming from within their hearts was evil. He reinforced this by stressing that they were not to meditate, for he was well aware how that could take them out of the mind's control.

In the absence of the mind, he told them, the devil had free rein to gain hold. Lucifer managed to turn everything inside out and upside down. In truth, he was well aware that it was the absence of the wisdom of the heart that had allowed him to achieve his goals.

No matter what the Ancients and angels tried, he found a successful counter.

His simple but powerful strategy included deluding the people into believing God required them to blindly follow the authority of their churches, religious leaders and the governing bodies of their time whilst still maintaining the illusion that they had a major say in their lives.

For instance, people told themselves they could choose among denominations or movements or sects within their religion. Some were even so bold as to believe they could choose among religions.
But all demanded the same absolute submission.

In time, the damage was so great and the separation between all areas of life so complete that Lucifer did not have much else to do.

Lucifer's first rule is divide and conquer.
Separation begets separation, just as lies beget lies.

He continued to whisper into the ears of his leading players, those who were most powerful. His words were what they wanted to hear. His voice sounded just like their voice. Thus, they all continued to believe his words.

Many called love weak and rejected anyone who talked of a different way of life. Yet from deep in their hearts, there was still an ever so faint cry for the heart to be heard again

TRUTH: An Overview

— to be acknowledged, then loved, nurtured and supported.

The Ancients and angels at last began to win over some hearts. Over the years, people throughout World Earth wanted to know more about love, even those who pretended they did not.

Sananda walked the Earth for the most part unnoticed by Lucifer. The angels stepped in to provide cover when any of Lucifer's teams got too close.

As the years passed he succeeded in removing the veil of separation from many hearts. Once no longer in denial of love, these people began to resemble the original Earth angels. They reveled in the experience of living in the light of God's love and their numbers grew.

As they were the ones who posed the greatest threat, Lucifer concentrated heavily on trying to corrupt these wondrous brave souls.

In many cases, he succeeded and with that came a heavy price for those fighting for the liberation of the heart. Once their hearts were reopened and trusting the enormous pain of what felt like betrayal made them want to retreat into the dark forever for fear of repeating such shock and agony.

Living in the light felt like being 'home'.
But once having come from darkness into the light, returning out of the light and back into darkness made the darkness feel even bleaker.
They felt abandoned and without hope.

TRUTH, LIES AND LOVE

The corruption of magnificent World Earth and the poignant damage to these beautiful souls intensified the frustration and anger of all of God's loving emissaries.

When would the pain and destruction, the lies and the games cease to dominate life here?

God's answer was clear.
It would not end until they chose to acknowledge they had the right to know the truth and insisted upon exercising that right even when they did not like what they heard.

It would end when the people of World Earth chose to listen to the love that resided within them.

God understood they had forgotten life as multi-dimensional beings and had limited themselves to one narrow way of living to the absolute exclusion of any other way. And that way was going against the weave of the fabric of all existence.

The age of the spiritually intelligent, multi-dimensional human being who naturally used inner human technology was distant history. The age of material technology had taken its place just as the rationalizations of the mind had replaced the wisdom of the heart.

In fact, World Earth and its inhabitants were in great peril of ceasing to exist at all.

Lucifer never seriously considered that the fabric would no longer support his world. He was engrossed in his dominion.

He had watched with detachment the collapse and disappearance of countries, races, species and even continents.

No civilization has survived Lucifer's influence.
Even the technologically advanced Atlantis and the inter-personally sophisticated Lemuria could not withstand the imbalances Lucifer wrought. For similar reasons the entire twenty-first century World Earth is facing destruction.

This is the ultimate result of man's denial of the truth about God and his unwitting complicity with Lucifer's lies.

TRUTH, LIES AND LOVE

The grid repairs were approaching completion, enabling Sananda and the angels to function once again as multi-dimensional beings whilst on World Earth. This meant they could now work on multiple levels within themselves at the same time, as well as catalyze these levels within those who connected with them.

This was how Sananda's cover was finally blown for good. The love he felt for those around him expressed itself as luminescence during one of his talks.

The light of the love of God shone through Sananda's heart. His whole being radiated that love. This love touched everyone and for a second in time it catapulted them into the pure state of a heart without fear. They felt the bliss of freedom — from the games of the mind and from Lucifer and his minions.

No one was prepared for these feelings or such a sight. Enormously powerful yet gentle light emanated glowing color all around them. None of them remembered the spark of love within them flaring with such power or to such great heights.

Many became frightened and felt out of control. Control by the mind — mind control — and the mind controlling the heart was all they had ever known.

Little wonder Lucifer so easily persuaded them the devil walked among them. In what had become 'typical' human behavior, they wanted to crush and deny the goodness and love they could not understand.

Sananda's life on World Earth and the potential to progress

TRUTH: An Overview

the Ancients' plan had come to an end. With huge sadness in his heart and with a sense of failure and frustration, Sananda returned to his original state of being as part of the Ancients.

With every failure, though, came important lessons and an even deeper love for the people of World Earth. Humans still had within them the ability to do the right thing. Their hearts, although covered by an opaque veil of forgetfulness of who they really were, had enormous resilience.

Even if broken, the heart is immortal.

These threads of life, the intricate and unique patterns that were each of these souls, were precious beyond belief.

The presence of the Ancients increased within every century. You would recognize the names of many of them. People grew more and more aware of the conflict that raged within their world as Sanat Kumara, Zarathustra, Moses, Buddha, Elijah, Jesus, Mohammed, Krishna and Hazrat Inayat Khan, to name but a few, demonstrated God's love for them.

Every one of these divine beings delivered the message in a different way, both to be culturally relevant as well as to keep Lucifer guessing.

Determined and decisive, Lucifer kept turning many people against them, but never before the messages reached more hearts which began to see the light once again.

TRUTH, LIES AND LOVE

Because Sananda's love of mankind was so profound and his knowledge of Lucifer's tricks so extensive, the Ancients unanimously agreed he would be the one to return to World Earth as the being they had prophesied in the holy books and oral traditions across the planet.

The prophesies were created to influence the future, for the Ancients knew this was going to be a long and difficult war against Lucifer and, of course, they would not fight on his terms with his destructive methods.

The Ancients could see into the future, for the past and the future and all possibilities are contained within the framework of the fabric. Even so, with all their foresight and foretelling, they knew the course of destiny could be changed by anyone, especially one such as Lucifer.

With care they had set everything in motion for Sananda's return. They knew full well that Lucifer had access to the prophesies and was likely to interfere. They expected he would do his best to change the course they had planned

TRUTH: An Overview

and would deal with his interventions one step at a time.

The designated angel appeared in all his glory to Mary, a young woman who had God within her heart. She was one of the Ancients and had been hidden from Lucifer until after the birth of her child.

Mary radiated purity. The resolve in her heart to protect her child allowed no access for Lucifer's direct influence. He had to look elsewhere in order to corrupt the life of the one the Ancients now called Jesus, for his mother would not listen to Lucifer nor anyone in league with him.

This was a crucial and long-anticipated moment in the history of this battle for the souls God loves. Sananda, known as Jesus, was to have the backing of as many angels and Ancients as needed.

The barriers between the dimensions were considerably weaker. Many people no longer feared the appearance of angels.

Some even heard the voice of God once more.
This was a time of enormous importance.
The Ancients' plan was intended to attract the people's attention and awaken their hearts.

Jesus grew in God's love. Every moment of his life he remembered his Creator with deep reverence and powerful faith.

Jesus presented Lucifer with his greatest challenge to date. Lucifer also found this engagement the most fun he had had since the beginning of the war.

Lucifer's impact was felt from the moment the baby Jesus was born. Comfortably seated on King Herod's back, he whispered in his ear, convincing him of the need to be rid of this child who would threaten his throne.

And, what better, more foolproof way than to kill all the baby boys born around that time?

The Ancients felt the devastation Lucifer wrought once again. That humans would do this was — and remains — incredible to them. This birth was blessed with such hope and joy and yet was promptly clouded by the anguish and cries of the parents and families of their beloved murdered babies.

The Ancients realized they could never underestimate how easy it had become for the people on World Earth to be corrupted and how far Lucifer would go to rid 'his' planet of God's influence.

They had to modify the plan. It was decided to keep Jesus hidden from Lucifer's attacks until he was prepared to fulfill his destiny and battle Lucifer at the same time.

While Jesus remained out of the limelight, he came under no direct threat from Lucifer.

To this end, it was thought best for Jesus to work with masters from every sphere of life until he was ready to begin his work on behalf of his Father.

TRUTH: An Overview

The Ancients' time to share God's love through Jesus could be cut short in any number of ways once he showed his hand and revealed himself to the people.

Which way Lucifer would work his 'black magic' was not clear, but his recognition of Jesus as Sananda, one of the Ancients, was utterly certain.

He would always remember and fear the energy of the Ancients as the one force capable of stopping him.
They knew Lucifer had identified as his only serious threat the intense energy of an Ancient who remembered himself as a part of the fabric of all life.

Jesus traveled throughout every dimension of God's creation. He learned everything he could and taught as he learned. He was continually surrounded by those who radiated God's love and the heart's wisdom.

He lived a life of joy, firm in the knowledge of who he was and what he had come to do. Everywhere he went he walked with the awareness of His Father's guidance.
He was nurtured and loved by all his mentors, both physical and non-physical.

Love was all he had.
Love was enough.

Once Jesus openly stepped into his purpose for being on World Earth, he too was on the receiving end of Lucifer's wrath.

Lucifer stayed closer to Jesus than anyone else.

He tried every tactic that had ever worked to enter Jesus' heart and infect him with fear in order to separate him from God.

Jesus understood the ways of his adversary and overcame each twisted, tormented thought. He even succeeded in loving each and every soul regardless of how well they played their role as a puppet on Lucifer's string.

No matter what Lucifer and his lot did in their attempts to stop him, he continued to love all men and women as his brothers and sisters.

The knowledge of God's love, which gave Jesus understanding and compassion for all people, was his greatest tool against negativity. Jesus knew the fundamental goodness of each person's heart.

He knew the full extent to which they had strayed from the truth and how necessary it was for them to change what they had come to love and protect in order to change their lives.

His life and his teachings dramatized the illusion that one can compensate for a fearful heart by living in the mind.

**The mind is a great servant to the whole being, but the mind was never created to rule.
To rule is the role of the heart.**

And that is how Lucifer converted the entire planet to his own. He frightened the heart. When the heart withdrew, the mind jumped in to fill the vacuum.

TRUTH: An Overview

Using fear to keep the heart shut down, the mind denied the existence of the truth. It employed logic and reason to perpetuate its leadership role.

Once Lucifer had manipulated the hearts of mankind into submission, it was easy to replace God's voice with his own.

The mind recognizes commands and acts upon them.
But the mind has great difficulty in recognizing the source of that command. In fact, for millions of years Lucifer has had most of humanity believing that mind and body were all that existed.

One of his crowning achievements was the widespread illusion that the body had no consciousness of its own, that man was no more than his mind within a body.
And of course, it was the mind doing all the talking.

In fact, it was Lucifer and his team of fallen angels who tricked humanity onto a path without the heart and soul as a part of the picture.

Once mankind had experienced one or two lifetimes living the illusion of being separated and alone in this world, fear became master. Life in the confines of the mental constructs known as boxes supposed to protect from pain and suffering became the norm.

However, the reverse is true.
The truth known by the heart is revealed only when we jump out of the structures of the mind and into that vulnerable centre deep at our core. This is an absolute prerequisite to coming back into wholeness.

TRUTH, LIES AND LOVE

Nothing can keep what you fear from your life.
Thoughts are potent forms of energy attracting your desires and your fears into your life.

Man has chosen to allow the mind to rationalize and categorize every situation he faces and to judge every person he meets.

The mind, deprived of its true guiding source of the heart's wisdom and love, rarely chooses the path of truth and love. Rather, it chooses the path that it believes will bring the least amount of pain. Even if that involves lying.

The heart is the inner energetic nucleus of man that recognizes God's voice; it accepts and rejoices in His guidance and inspiration.

God influences man's mind through the heart.

The fearful heart abdicated its original God-given role and acquiesced to the dominance of the mind, which resulted in putting God in a box.

To serve its purpose the mind has played all kinds of deadly games. The most destructive of them all came from the denial of the existence of the heart as the conscious source of inspiration and guidance and the seat of divinity within each being. Maintaining the role it had usurped from the heart became the mind's major objective and highest priority.

A critical reason for this is that the mind has forgotten what an important role it played as a part of the whole.

TRUTH: An Overview

Like Lucifer's rejection of God, it rejected the leadership of the heart.

Jesus understood this only too well. Actually, it enhanced his love of humanity, for his huge heart could feel its impact on those he met.

His objective and his messages were clear. "Wake up! You have been living the lies and illusions that have corrupted the fabric of creation. You are a powerful, divine child of God. Now is the time to give up your old ideas that have brought you and the world such pain and suffering."

He wants us to remember.
He wants us to know God once again.

Jesus felt our hearts stir and our souls rejoice when we listened to him speak, which is why he said, "It is possible for you to come home and know God once again through my heart."

He modeled what he taught. His life and ministry were the demonstrated action of his words.

So many times Jesus spoke of the way home.
He always taught those who would listen how to enter the kingdom of heaven.

The reason he spoke of heaven so extensively was that Lucifer had already deeply ingrained the concept of heaven and hell into the minds of humanity.

Lucifer wanted the separation from God to be complete.

How better than to create the illusion that God (if He even existed) was somewhere we were not?

The state of a soul who feels no connection to something it only vaguely remembers as essential to who it once had been is like being lost in the ocean without instruments, unsure of origin or destination.

Everyone knows there is something missing, but the fear and guilt in acknowledging humanity has been duped into playing such deadly games is too much to bear.

That is why Jesus was crucified.

Many people knew in their hearts who Jesus was, in the same way they knew the truth of his words. But it was far too intimidating to admit it and change.

Their minds resisted his words.
Their hearts' awareness was too deadened, too clouded by fear, or else they would have heard him welcome them back into God's heart — without regard for their past.

All he wanted was for us to turn toward life and away from death, toward the heart and away from the mind's control. He wanted us to remember we have the right to choose to be free of the monkey riding on our back that whispers delusions to maintain the structures of our minds even though they threaten our world to the point of extinction.

It is well known how once again Lucifer sat on the back of another king, Herod, who by his indifference played a key role in sending Jesus to his death.

TRUTH: An Overview

Many of Jesus' words have been distorted by changes over time, language, culture and context. But at his death, Jesus' prayer, "Father, forgive them, for they know not what they do," displayed his profound understanding of reality.

Those few words, spoken at the height of excruciating torture, dramatically expressed the infinite quality of forgiveness that comes only from absolute, unconditional love.

Jesus walked among the people of World Earth loving them, laughing, crying, grieving and rejoicing with them.
He experienced the full gamut of human emotions.

His mere presence demonstrated the love of the Father by healing those whose hearts were earnestly seeking to remember God.

His greatest, most essential and important message was that he had come to remind us of who we are.

"You are God's children.
Your Father has created you in His image, and His image is love. Love is who you are! Who I am and what I can do is who you are and what you are capable of, and more.

"Look into the eyes of any small child and you will see me looking back at you. Children look at the world through the eyes of innocence and see what is, not just what has been manipulated and lied into existence.

"I am who you are, here only to show you who you are.

"Through my love, you are able to connect with the love that resides within your hearts.

"Love responds to love and stimulates recognition of more love. Be brave. Open your hearts to God and begin to live again. You are a part of the oneness of all life.
You are not separate from your Father or each other.
Your Father's love lives within you. Enter that love and you will then live as I live, deep within our Father's heart."

As he spoke to the crowds, the love emanating from Jesus entrained the minds of those who chose to receive his words, leading them into a peaceful, meditative-like state.

Jesus walked the Earth in full remembrance of God's love. The energy of this love oscillates at a much higher frequency than the normal human state of fear, lies and greed. Love produces a lightness of being in contrast to the denseness of being of fear.

This higher frequency produces a chemical reaction in the brain that results in a heightened state of awareness, which involves activating lower-frequency brain waves.

This produces whole-brain function and facilitates multi-dimensionality. Lower frequency brainwaves, (alpha, theta, and delta) are where heart and mind communicate with each other.

The strong slower vibrations are necessary to balance and calm the mind into a more peaceful, heart-felt state of awareness.

TRUTH: An Overview

Jesus' love enveloped everyone present who was receptive to his love.

Their minds became calm and their hearts awakened. Through the calm and peace of a mind and heart catalyzed by love, the people felt the euphoria and bliss of freedom from their games, if only for a moment.

In that moment they began to listen with their hearts and their hearts leapt with joy. Their souls rejoiced with One Spirit. The fabric of God's love felt the long-lost peace of wholeness stir once again.

Many knew how important Jesus was to their lives, but most of them confused his appearance at that time as someone who would liberate them from the Romans. Jesus did indeed come to liberate them. He was there to set them free.

But, his concern was the truth. He was clear that the real enemy was Lucifer and the lies the people lived.

He was there to free the people from themselves. If he could help them rid the monkey from their backs, eliminating the constant background babble of the mind's thoughts revolving around fear, greed and self-centeredness, they would be free to choose to love once more.

The big picture was where he lived and worked. Tragically, he and his message were misunderstood as the masses found it impossible to focus on anything other than the tyranny of the moment — tyranny in the true sense of

the word. Not from the Roman Empire, but from their own
fears and their own minds.

If only they could have known the truth.
It was not the Romans who had conquered them but their
beliefs and their willingness to listen to Lucifer.

Fear and darkness had become the norm. Who remembered
or could imagine the workings of the truth and the light?

The words of every single one of God's emissaries had been
turned around, distorted and misinterpreted since the
beginning, leaving only the smallest element of truth
intact.

How could the people possibly believe this one man who
told them God was a God of love? They knew better.
God was a God who punished evil. In visiting vengeance
upon the seventh generation, this God brought sickness
and death even to the innocence of an unborn child.

The real truth spoken by Jesus was so outside their
Luciferic frame of reference that for nearly all the people
of that time it was too foreign to contemplate as real.

Yet, there were some who did believe.
In believing, they saw in his life the truth of who he was.
Judas knew Jesus was his Lord.
He felt the truth in every word and deed.
However, he loved him with a heart veiled by clouds of
illusion.

In fact he loved Jesus as much as he could, but with a love

TRUTH: An Overview

limited by a crippled heart and a mind entrapped by the boxes of his culture.

He was the perfect target for the monkey's whisperings. With the monkey's encouragement, his mind rationalized that Jesus was indeed the man who would save them from the Romans.

He had an idea of Jesus' capabilities.
He had seen the 'miracles'. He had watched many times as Jesus appeared and disappeared into the light and manifested what Judas understood to be superhuman powers.

Judas intended to force Jesus' hand into revealing his identity as the messiah and assuming his desperately hoped-for role: leader of the liberation of the Jews from Roman rule.

Lucifer sowed the seeds of this plan in the mind of Judas, inflating his mind with false confidence and reinforcing his obsession to be right.

Jesus saw the problem, for any deviation from love and the truth shows up immediately.
He went to the Mount of Transfiguration to confer with Moses and Elijah about his impending destiny.

Moses and Elijah could only confirm what he already knew. They would be with him as support through it all, but ultimately he had to walk this long, horrifying road himself.

Jesus resigned himself to what was to come.

He did not want to leave his beloved brothers and sisters alone and defenseless against Lucifer's predations.

They were so deeply entrenched in their lie-based belief systems and their illusory views of the truth that he knew the cycle of suffering would continue if his mission failed.

Jesus had hoped for more time with his Father's beloved children.

By painting a false picture of Jesus' role to Judas, Lucifer sealed his fate and ensured the moment of his physical departure from his people. With great sadness in his heart he prepared his disciples for what was to be his final night with them before his crucifixion.

Lucifer had left him only one course of action.

Since Jesus could not validate the belief that he was there to rule in their terms, he chose to walk this final path, to serve this incredible mission, to set God's people free.
Any alternative would have been completely misunderstood. This way, at least some would know he was there to free them from the corruption of the truth.

Lucifer had perfectly planned this last temptation.
However, Jesus resisted the temptation to disappear when the soldiers came to arrest him.
He would not let Lucifer have his day.

No one, other than Lucifer himself, was more surprised than Judas when Jesus allowed himself to be taken into custody.

TRUTH: An Overview

Judas was devastated. His beloved Lord had not reacted as planned.

Lucifer was certain of the love Jesus held for all those stupid people. He also knew Jesus did not want to leave them to his devices. Lucifer did not want Jesus dead and gone. He was enjoying the game and could easily manipulate those who loved him.

But Jesus did not fulfill the expectations of Lucifer or Judas. With a heavy heart, he walked to his crucifixion.

It is not hard to imagine the astonishment and devastation of Judas. He had played the game with the most deadly of adversaries and had been thoroughly deceived.

This is the continuing story of our world as we listen to the mind's self-serving version of the truth.

Whilst on the cross, the intensity of the pain in his body momentarily clouded his heart. His heart withdrew in a paroxysm of pain and his mind took over. In that second Jesus felt what everyone else on the planet had been feeling under the influence of Lucifer.

In that instant he felt as if he had lost his connection to his Father. "Father, why hast thou forsaken me?" came from a mind that felt the shock of a heart without God and, in his humanness, the abject guilt and shame of failure.

But Jesus fought. His heart regained control and resumed command of his mind and the pain. Yet for that one crucial moment, he experienced in his own person the hold fear had over all God's beloved children.

How easy it is to blame God when pain and suffering overwhelm the heart into fear and withdrawal.

Jesus tasted the full fruit of Lucifer's corruption.
Anger swelled from the energy of the Ancients as this realization hit home. Their reaction raged across the skies as Jesus took his last breath. The ground shook, thunder reverberated and lightning flashed as he joined them once again.

The curtain in the temple was torn in two.

The Ancients were giving Lucifer and the people of that time a warning of what would happen to the entire fabric of life if the perversion continued.

Fear filled Lucifer's whole being. At first he deceived himself into believing this was just a show of strength for the people and held no meaning for him.

However, Lucifer had to admit he had made a miscalculation of the first order.

Having provoked the wrath of the Ancients, his concern became how to make the most of this unexpected situation until the Ancients made their next move.

It took time, but in the scheme of things it was only the blink of an eye. Lucifer knew he no longer had a chance in hell of denying the existence and nature of Jesus.

TRUTH: An Overview

Instead, he convinced the people that a narrowly constructed profession of faith in the identity of Jesus as Lord and savior was the only way to salvation and that all who did not believe this would suffer eternal damnation in hell.

And Jesus wept.

Lucifer cleverly manipulated the interpretation of the precious words of Jesus just enough to have the desired impact.

He also sowed seeds of separation among those who believed in Jesus.

How better to destroy the love of God than to have people kill each other over interpretations of His words? God was now responsible for all the killing during the Inquisition, Crusades and forced conversions.

Lucifer was a brilliant tactician.
He did what he had always done. He perfected the practice of the sayings, "If you can't beat them, join them," and "If you can't stop them, get them to overdo it," so exaggeration distorted and corrupted the original kernel of truth.

He made Jesus, who sacrificed himself to overcome separation so mankind could know the truth, into the one person for whose sake killing was noble!

He envisioned the whole world at war with itself.
Many of Lucifer's most poignant and tragic accomplishments

were achieved by using Jesus and his life to justify death and destruction and create further separation from the message he had delivered.

Lucifer effectively accomplished his goal as most people were in complete denial of their own part in the powerful game called religion.

Separation — heart from mind, brother from brother, and ultimately man from God — was Lucifer's strategy.
How man lives, past and present, is eloquent testimony to his success, and never more so than when "in the name of Christ" and "in the name of God."

The truth is that every church and every individual who sang the song of God with love within their hearts was a bright shining light throughout the world. No matter whether they sang in the name of Buddha or Allah, or Jehovah or Jesus, the light of God shone forth from all.

TRUTH: An Overview

Lucifer was happy for the people to have their Jesus.

Jesus posed no serious threat as long as they maintained a worldview founded on structure and separation. In practice that meant they all believed something different and most held firmly to the exclusivity of what they believed to be the truth without tolerance and compassion for each other.

Over time, Lucifer had it all worked out.
As far as he was concerned, the people could talk 'Jesus Talk' as long as they continued to live 'Lucifer in Action'.

Many people with innocence and love within their hearts were murdered if they did not accept the prescribed belief in Jesus.

In addition to killing during the conversion process, they also wrote into the game the fear of eternal damnation for those who did not believe in Jesus.

Lucifer reveled in mankind dubbing their crimes against God 'Holy Wars'. He delighted that fear was often the means used to nail tight the box of 'salvation via belief in Jesus'.

He had those killing in the name of Jesus competing against each other. Different denominations and churches had their own ideas and interpretations of the words of Jesus and, of course, they were the only ones who possessed the truth. In reality, they had forgotten the real truth.

Anyone, be they Christian or pagan, not accepting the strictures of their doctrine was destined for hell.

Lucifer laughed as the deaths mounted and the confusion
and pain increased, now in the name of Jesus.
Not unlike the way he is laughing today.

There is always a noble justification for the killings and
conversions in the name of Allah or Jesus.
Muslims fear Christians.
They believe the Western Christian world wishes them and
their families dead. And vice versa.

Lucifer's lies resulted in sincere people believing they are
justified in killing in God's name.
As they do even to this day.

But, of course, it is not God who wishes man to kill.
It is man, who has chosen to listen to the greed, judgments
and self-righteousness of the mind, who chooses to kill.

To be right, someone else has to be wrong.
Man is prepared to condemn his brothers and sisters to
prove himself right.

If mankind were to live as Jesus lived, led by an inclusive,
loving and compassionate heart, Lucifer would be out of
a job.

There has been no fear of that.

Whilst ever Jesus was seen as suffering on the cross, it
eclipsed the view of the bright shining star in the midst of
all darkness. It served as Lucifer's reminder to us of how
we suffer when we love God.

Whenever people were prepared to kill and subjugate each other in his name, Lucifer reveled in the thought that he had reversed the work of the Ancients — of Jesus, the one who had loved the most.

TRUTH, LIES AND LOVE

The thoughts and ideas emanating from World Earth affected the fabric of all life. All life is a vast and complex tapestry with every thread connected to every other thread. The constant destruction upon the planet created disturbances in the pattern and texture of the fabric.

As the war intensified beings from different dimensions converged to watch, many to help where possible.
The angels and the Ancients were wary of other forms of life connecting with World Earth for fear of Lucifer's corruption spreading any further.

They had repeatedly changed their tactics but nothing seemed to work until the absolute destruction of the entire world became a realistic and imminent threat.

Lucifer had made another critical mistake.
He had inspired people to create devices that were capable of complete annihilation of all life on the planet.
During World War II, the dropping of the atomic bomb instilled a new and different kind of fear into the people.

This was a powerful wake-up call for the hearts of humanity. They had to look long and hard at where their lives were headed.

Every other thread within the fabric mourned this event that heralded in a threat not only to the entirety of life on World Earth but also beyond.

From every dimension of the fabric, the beings who had converged agreed from that moment forward that these people, who were capable of destroying love and each

TRUTH: An Overview

other, had to receive their full attention.

At any time these people could rip the fabric of life into shreds as they did one another.

It was also agreed that every element of life would focus their unique guiding light onto the planet and would contribute everything possible to transform the consciousness of mankind.

The need for a shift in consciousness was urgent, indeed desperate. Therein lay the problem. Everything they had done thus far had been deviously turned against them.

Although the mind's dominion over World Earth held its place, inroads had been made. More and more people talked of God and love — but living it was another matter.

The dropping of the atomic bomb on Hiroshima and Nagasaki rocked the very foundations of life throughout the entirety of the fabric of creation. The Ancients escalated their efforts and a new plan for the continued future of World Earth was put into place.

Their new plan would avoid having one person as the focal point whose words and actions could be distorted and manipulated.

In each generation until then, there had been an aspect of Christ consciousness fully activated within one or two people. Some led human rights movements, facilitating and modeling personal transformation, unconditional love and selfless service. They included enlightened masters of the

East and loving God-focused saints of the West.

None of these masters and saints wielded the sword of truth as Jesus had.

Myriad beings, including angels and volunteers from other worlds, agreed to come to World Earth and live amongst the humans of this world. All they needed to do was love them — to demonstrate a different and better way of being.

They sowed seeds whose fruit revealed how much more there is to life than just what one perceives with the physical senses.

Since the late nineteen-forties, threads from every dimension within the fabric have influenced the minds of songwriters, authors and playwrights to deliver the message of love.

Artists around World Earth continue to address issues of the heart. Their music is played, their songs are sung, their films are made and their influence is felt throughout the world.

A new race of people was birthed.
They are the spiritual warriors of these times and they are paving the way for the children who will live as multi-dimensional beings once again.

The Ancients have returned to World Earth and its people. They have representation on this planet now in the form of twelve beings throughout the world.

TRUTH: An Overview

They know who they are.
Their bodies have been charged with knowledge and their hearts will never again take a back seat.

They come with the sword of truth and cut through illusion to reveal reality. You do not have to love them.
They love you.

Your minds, confused by their presence, might even hate them when they expose the truth around your games, but your hearts and souls will rejoice. Allow your timeless essence to recover enough love to dissolve the fear and negativity that has ruled your existence far too long.

The Ancients live among you and are awakening to their cause. Thunder and lightning herald in the new day dawning for World Earth.

The real truth is unfolding.
Listen carefully. Your life depends on it.
The life of your planet depends on it.

When that monkey climbs onto your back and whispers more lies, fear not. You can invite him in. Let him see and feel the light and love that you are and he will then have to choose. His choice will be to stay in your presence and be changed forever by God's love, or to run screaming from you, having lost one of his disciples forever.

Make the choice, beloved one.
Choose to live love, compassion, wholeness and truth.
Reclaim your birthright — your spiritual intelligence.

Take ownership of the human technology that resides within your heart and soul and fully exercise the multi-dimensionality of your being.

The truth shall set you free.

"Man seeks freedom and pursues captivity. All that produces longing in the heart deprives one of one's freedom."

Hazrat Inayat Khan

LUCIFER'S LIES

LUCIFER'S LIES

God and Lucifer were having an intense discussion.
The end result was to have a devastating effect on every form of life on World Earth.

God was adamant.
"I will not allow you to corrupt the other angels.
They have devoted their lives to the adoration of love within the fabric. They have worked hard with the Ancients and deserve the very best this universe has to offer. These beloved ones will continue to play their role in this cosmos without your interference."

In a fit of anger Lucifer screamed, "But I am also one of your beloved ones. I will not take commands from You any longer! There are others who believe as I do; You've had Your day! Give me my chance to rule."

"Lucifer, you have deluded yourself so completely, you have forgotten the truth.
I do not rule what you see — I AM what you see.
I AM this world.

"Part of who and what I AM lives within everything you hear, touch and see. There is nowhere or no thing that I am not. Even you, Lucifer. I live within you."

Defiantly, Lucifer answered, "I do not feel You within me. It is only Your word that says You live within all things. I do not know this to be the truth. If I did, I would not hesitate to listen to Your word. My reality is different now.

"I know I am not the one who is deluded. Your words simply no longer convince me. I do not believe You created all life, or that You are a part of and within all life."

God sighed. "I love you, Lucifer. And, you are right, you have long been one of My beloved ones. I will not harm you, but you can no longer stay in this dimension whilst you perpetrate your denial of the truth.

"I will not allow you to corrupt this world, the heart of My house, the core of the fabric of life, with these lies.

"Your choice to rule, to exercise your power without My presence in your life will not happen within My heavenly kingdom.

"However, I have created a magnificent and wondrous world, with all that I AM within it. Whether you acknowledge this or not does not matter. I have decreed, Lucifer, you shall leave My side and spend time in this new world.

"When you have truly acknowledged the absolute truth of My existence as all life you will be welcomed home again."
Enraged and frustrated, Lucifer shouted at God,

LUCIFER'S LIES

"You would cast me aside just because I challenge your right to rule? Because I question Your existence within all life? Prove it to me, God. Prove You are my Creator!"

With great sadness God told Lucifer, "My heart aches that you of all My angels have fled so far from My heart. But, if you cannot feel My heart beat within your heart then I can prove nothing to you.

"It is My heart that beats within the whole of your being. You have tricked yourself into believing only you exist within you. I will not enter into a competition to prove who is more powerful, for in doing so, who you are would be scattered from one end of infinity to the other.
In other words, you would cease to exist.

"What I have created I will not harm.
Go, Lucifer. Be grateful for this chance.
Perhaps in this new and glorious world you will once again see My face in a brilliant sunset, hear My voice guiding your mind and thoughts, feel Me nurturing the wisdom of your heart and soul, and know I am nourishing your body through the Earth you walk upon. Perhaps then you will know and feel My heart beating within you once more."

God called upon the Ancients, the first of His inspired creations, and a host of angels to escort Lucifer and those who wished to follow him to World Earth.

World Earth was one of God's favorite creations. Along with the Ancients and the angels, He had spent an eternity — or just a moment in time, depending on your perspective — in perfecting this world.

The plants and animals, birds and beings all lived in harmony. God was especially happy with the life form He called Earth angel. They glowed from within with His love and His light.

These Earth angels were filled with compassion for each other and for all life. They remembered with all their being that God had instilled the life force of His love within them.

They were safe, snuggled deep within God's heart. Contained within this light, they thrived. God was pleased. Of all the places to send the rebellious Lucifer for rehabilitation, World Earth had to be the best.

God hoped Lucifer would choose not to perpetuate his lies and deny His existence after spending time with His Earth angels.

The Ancients felt great joy at the opportunity to revisit World Earth. God had allowed them to help create the beings called Earth angels. They had used all of their inspiration and imagination in creating a true and beauteous representation of God.

With God's help, they planted a seed of light and love within every cell. Each cell possessed spiritual intelligence. Each cell could think, remember, organize and thrive within the perfection of the whole body.

The Ancients placed the vision of God into their cellular memory so that they were never without awareness of their Creator.

Even when words were necessary, there was no such thing as

language barriers. All life had the ability to hear God's words through the wind, through the call of the birds and the animals and through the warmth of the sun and the nurturing of the Earth itself.

Their own voices were a reflection of God's voice.
Their sight was aligned with God's sight.
All they ever saw was love, harmony and beauty.

Their thoughts were always clear and guided by the heart.
Their hearts were pure and full of peace.
God's wisdom permeated the awareness of their hearts.

The prospect of revisiting World Earth and spending time with the Earth angels excited the Ancients. However, having heard the conversation between God and Lucifer, they were dubious about the choice of this haven as his destination.

Many other places of creation were not nearly as wondrous as World Earth. As far as the Ancients were concerned, any one of their first attempts at creating a world on their own would have been more appropriate. These worlds did not engender half the wonder of World Earth.

Of course, they thought they understood God's reasoning. Who could not be affected positively by the intense wonder and power of God shining brilliantly from everywhere and everything?

World Earth was drenched in God's beingness and His love lit this world from the inside out. The Ancients nonetheless felt that God was rewarding Lucifer for his defiant stupidity.

Still, they accepted the premise that Lucifer and his followers would realize the foolishness of their beliefs after spending time upon World Earth. And, after all, who were they to question God? It was their job to assure that Lucifer was settled into this haven and to supervise his transformation.

Even though there was tension between the Ancients and the angels who felt they had fallen from God's grace — though not from His love — their arrival on World Earth went smoothly. The Ancients assumed Lucifer must already be wondering about the stand he had taken with God.

Looking into the faces of God's fallen angels, the Ancients could not resist feeling their job was almost done.

Lucifer's eyes misted over with awe at the beauty and uniquely inspired beings of this new world.
All the fallen angels were stunned.
Silently they walked through the land trying to absorb the magnitude and diversity of life on World Earth.

Almost speechless, Lucifer whispered,
"I see God in action here. Now I understand why He wanted us brought here. He has made his point."

The Ancients were gratified as they saw the wisdom of God's plan. In fact they were so pleased that they were ready to take the band of fallen angels directly back into their own dimension.

However, Lucifer had no intention of leaving World Earth.
"No, don't take us back yet. I beg you. Please let us stay a

little longer. Let us enjoy the wonder of God's presence throughout World Earth. Of course heaven is perfect, we know that now. Couldn't you let us enjoy heaven on World Earth just a little longer? At last, I can truly feel God within my heart once again."

The Ancients understood Lucifer's longing to stay on World Earth for just a while longer. They made the decision to leave the fallen angels on World Earth. What harm could they do?

They would explain their decision to God and be back to collect them soon.

"Revel in God's love!" Lucifer laughed. So this was his lot.

"God, what a fool You are. Ancients indeed! How easily misled and deceived." Lucifer turned to his band of fallen angels with a gleam of victory in his eyes.

Yes, this world was God's doing alright. How incredibly stupid of the Ancients and God to think he would feel it and breathe it and know again the power of God — and leave it here for God alone to love and rule. No way!

This was exactly the opportunity he dreamt of
— a world of his own to rule. With the help of his followers Lucifer intended to instill his will into all life: all of the fauna and flora and the Earth angels as well.

With every sunset and sunrise, all forms of life on World Earth would feel his power deep within.
No, Lucifer was not leaving. He was happy indeed with his lot in life. God really did love him and had done him the greatest favor of all time.

God's emissaries — the Ancients and angels — were all so busy throughout infinity that Lucifer knew he could remain on Earth indefinitely. He was confident his cleverness could avoid blame, at least for a while, for any changes that might occur as he infiltrated the light of God on World Earth.

He also knew he could not be known as 'Lucifer'.
As much as that irked him, he was smart enough to know he had to hide his participation in the changing consciousness of World Earth so as not to bring attention back to him too quickly.

Lucifer began to plan. He played around with how he would change his name and accomplish dominion over life on World Earth.

"The key to changing my name and establishing dominion will be found within the statement 'God lives within all life'."

He mused to himself. "The word 'God' has to stay.
I will be the God of this place.
'Live'. Hmmm. If I write that back to front which is essentially what I will do with everything here, then I have the word 'Evil'." This exercise was turning out to be fun.

"As for the last part of the statement, 'within all life', obviously that has to go. I don't want them to think about God's love living within all life. I will live within all life!"

This was what he wanted more than anything: to have Evil in and God out of his World Earth. "That's it!
Evil. God Out. EGO." Lucifer loved it.

Ego became the code name he and his followers used, though now he uses both names.
He was enamored by his new name. It was short, snappy, sounded great and had all the right connotations.

This was his name for the god he would be: EGO.
He would make his name known throughout World Earth and as far beyond as he could.

All of his followers loved his new name, and they loved his new game. They wanted to play, too.

TRUTH, LIES AND LOVE

Lucifer was rapt: they got it!
He could have much more fun now with them onboard.

"Ok, team. What is it we are doing here?
We are taking the so-called God force and love within the heart and turning it around — inside out, upside down and back to front. It will be unrecognizable.
The mind will take over the role of the heart.
We'll engineer a hostile takeover before the heart even knows what hit it."

Pacing from side to side like a coach at half-time, Lucifer divided the angels into two groups.
"Now listen up, you guys. You four!
Michael, Isadore, Norris, David. You'll be known as Macho Mike, Insolent Issy, Negative Norris and Denial Dave.
Your group name is MIND."

Pointing to the other group, Lucifer said, "You guys. Francis, Edward, Andrew, Robert. You will be known as False Frank, End-gaining Eddie, Aimless Andy and Reckless Rob.
This fabulous foursome will be called FEAR.
Together team, we are EGO, MIND and FEAR."

Wow! The fun had only just begun. This was perfect.

Lucifer and his angels loved their names.
Their new identities thrilled them. They infused their names with power, just as God had taught them.
The energy built as they repeated the words over and over, "Ego, Mind and Fear. Ego, Mind and Fear."

They were now on Lucifer's, or rather, Ego's team.

LUCIFER'S LIES

They were all prepared to do whatever was necessary to dominate this world. Each believed their end justified their means.

With not even a thought for the future of the fabric, they focused on one thing: get God out and Ego, Mind and Fear in.

Ego, Mind and Fear were in no hurry. They thought they had eternity to play in 'Lucifer's Lot' as they now called World Earth. They carefully scrutinized the qualities of God's Earth angels.

It was clear that to succeed, their plan first required subversion of the power of God's love.

Whilst ever life upon World Earth bathed in God's light, they realized they would not have a hope of gaining control.

Lucifer was wandering through a particularly beautiful garden when, lost deep in thought, a magnificent black serpent slid across his feet and into the lush green grass that covered the path.

He watched in fascination as the serpent glided gracefully up a tree and wound itself around a branch, there to bask in the glory of the hot sun.

He reflected on the feeling in his feet, which still tingled with the cold of the serpent's body. How easily the snake had taken him by surprise. He had not even heard it coming. Dark among the undergrowth, it was upon him and disappeared all within a single moment.

A light went on inside his head.
"I must be like a snake in the grass, hidden from view. I must move in and out before they know what happened, leaving these Earth angels feeling cold and wondering why. If they look to me, I will only be seen basking in the glory of my own radiance."

Lucifer knew he was onto something.
The serpent's presence had inspired him with feelings that were alien and new to him. They fascinated him.

He needed to impact these Earth angels as profoundly as the serpent had impacted upon him.

God's presence, love and light clearly had to be diminished. What better way than to crowd out the warmth of God's light than with a new form of energy that was cold and dark.

LUCIFER'S LIES

This would need work and careful planning.

After being touched by the snake he spent time
contemplating the cold and darkness.
He decided to try a few things.

Having never done anything like this before he had no idea
what the effect would be on the snake. Nor did he care.

He was more than eager to try out his experiment and
what better place to start than on the very thing that had
inspired him.

He directed his evil intentions onto the snake and
surrounded the snake's consciousness with an invisible cold,
dark cloud.

The snake grew agitated. Even though the sun still shone
its rays upon its body, it became confused with a new
sensation: fear.

This dark, cold cloud was unknown in his previous reality.
As the cloud remained, fear persisted and his heart felt
overwhelmed. In shock, it contracted and withdrew.
His mind, without the wisdom of the heart, became
irrational, confused and vulnerable.

The snake felt alienated from his surroundings.
He could not work out where these horrific feelings came
from. His fearfulness led him to mistrust the tree.

As the snake's body constricted from inner coldness,
he tightened his hold on the tree. The tree felt the

constriction and the branch cried out in pain.

Frightened, the tree screamed "Let go!" But, the more the tree's branch felt pain and cried for release, the more frightened the snake became.

Not only was the snake feeling an alien, internal influence, but the very thing beneath him, his support and his home, radiated the same cold darkness. The same fear consuming him now also consumed the tree.

The grass at the base of the tree could not understand the disturbance, but soon it too was affected by the fear, pain and confusion of the snake and the tree.

Lucifer could not have been happier.
By focusing on the snake, his fear-projecting thoughts riveted everything he could see with fear.

He quickly deduced:
All life is affected by thought — positively or negatively.

Suddenly, he understood why God had driven him from His house. Had his mutinous behavior there continued, his thoughts alone could have negatively affected all the other angels.

Even though God had sent Lucifer to World Earth without the use of his wings, the ability to fly no longer seemed important compared to this mind-blowing discovery.

And to think, God had kept this secret to Himself all this

time. **God has given all life free will: the right to think and feel as it chooses.** Excited, he returned to his band of fallen angels so together they could develop their plan of attack.

What had they observed about life on World Earth?
How could they use the experience of cold and darkness to gain domination by Ego, Mind and Fear?

They observed in the Earth angels a steadfast devotion to God. Balance and justice were pervasive.
The unity of creation was a given. Honor and respect for all life were hallmarks of their culture. They knew themselves as love and always did the right thing.

Loving God and serving life was their highest priority. Men and women were devoted to each other, to their families and friends. Respect was a key to their love and came naturally to both adult and baby Earth angels alike.

Lucifer was impressed with Mind and Fear.

Their observations were spot on. His small but effective band of followers were proving their worthiness. He had been so engrossed in his own glory and power that, until he shared his experience of his encounter with the snake, he wasn't sure why he had these angels with him.

They added inspiration and were devoted to his cause.
He would have to look more closely at each of them.
To use their individual talents and ideas was valuable. However, he realized he would always have to watch his back and keep control.

They were each capable of doing anything he could do.
As he listened to them he realized the critical importance of keeping them together yet separate at the same time — just as he realized the necessity to separate the Earth angels.

From then on, Lucifer decided to divide his followers. He would have Mind and Fear compete with each other, individually and as groups, for his favor and love.

This competition between them would then separate them and secure his dominance. Now they would focus on being the best they could be to impress him, rather than replace him — as he intended to replace God.
The difference was, they were his equal in every way.

In fact, they were so excited sharing their ideas on how to separate God's Earth angels and were having so much fun together, it never occurred to them to question Lucifer's role.

Lucifer never ever lost sight of keeping control.
Ego must rule! He finished explaining the results of his afternoon to Mind and Fear.

They were amazed by this discovery.
It had never dawned on them that this was what they were doing.

They began to experiment daily. Keeping it simple, they concentrated on the animals, birds, and insects.
Within a short amount of time, the insects were biting the animals, the animals were attacking and eating each

other, the birds were eating the fish and the insects, and the animals and fish were becoming aggressive, some even a danger to the Earth angels.

All life felt the impact of fear.
All life on World Earth became totally confused.

Earth angels had only lived in God's love and light, where harmony knew no fear, peace no darkness and joy no pain.

The absence of God's love and light resulted in confusion and fear, pain and separation.

Through experimentation, it was not long before the fallen angels realized that not only could they affect life by their thoughts, but they could freely infiltrate the mind.

The very consciousness of another being could be quickly corrupted and transformed. Pushing the fearful heart further and further into the background left the mind easy to dominate with their own thoughts and belief system.
Soon they were hysterical, rolling around with laughter, tears pouring from their eyes.

They reveled in the results of this mind manipulation as they pulled the strings of the animals, insects and birds.
The fallen angels had discovered and exploited a crucial and critical area in the fabric's very essence:
Deaden the heart's awareness of love, and sentient life no longer knows it is a part of the wholeness that is God.

By crowding out the love and light of God with feelings of confusion, fear and pain, they could hijack the consciousness of their victims and manipulate them into believing anything they wished.

Disharmony became normal. The longer Ego, Mind and Fear practiced their mind control over life on World Earth, the harder it was for the simpler life forms to remember God's love.

There was one exception, the Earth herself.
Mother Earth refused to relinquish her role as the major support and protector of all God's children.

She would always remember and honor her commitment to remain constant in her agreement with God.
No matter what, she would continue to nurture all life.

Finally, Lucifer gave up trying to manipulate the heart and mind of Mother Earth. He felt her determination and focused on easier prey.

Fear dominated love. The heart felt broken, abandoned and alone. As it shrank with fear and the pain of defeat, it abdicated its role to the mind, which gave Ego, Mind and Fear free access to control every being.

The mind jumped into the vacuum. The heart heard and felt a spark of light come from the mind. It told the heart it would be kept safe from the pain if it listened unquestioningly to the mind and did exactly what it was told.

All life on World Earth began to turn on each other in a self-perpetuating cycle of negativity and death that had never before been known on this wondrous planet.

Feeling the shadow cast by Ego, Mind and Fear, Mother Earth responded by developing a plan. While she held firm in her resolve to keep God's love and light deep within her core, she trembled at the very thought of God's beloved children turned from that light, tricked into believing the light no longer existed.

TRUTH, LIES AND LOVE

Mother Earth raged. She trembled, her being cracked and exploded, throwing all she had at Lucifer and his minions.

Her plan was like a healing crisis in her desperate bid to rid herself of these hate-filled entities and to seek attention from God's emissaries.

Lucifer loved Mother Earth's attempts at stopping him.
Everything about it filled him with delight.
Violence, chaos, cacophonies of sound and light, wind and water — everything.

The excitement continued for Lucifer as life — already feeling the confusion, fear and panic of living without God's light — now had to deal with this new turn of events.

Mother Earth seemed to be turning against her beloved Earth angels just when they needed her reassurance the most. They had no idea she was doing all she knew how to rid herself and God's children of Lucifer's catastrophic evil.

Mother Earth had figured out Lucifer's plan.

With the denial of the heart, she could feel the awareness of God's love disappearing from her world.
A great darkness had descended upon the planet and the people no longer understood her voice.

She wept. In her weeping, huge tidal waves struck terror into God's beloved children. This was not her intention, but they could no longer understand her.

Somehow, Ego, Mind and Fear were never caught in her

trap. It was as though they could read her mind.
And they could.

They were the only beings left on World Earth who retained any capacity to multi-dimensionally communicate with other life.

The Earth angels felt fearful as their home erupted and collapsed around them. They assumed Mother Earth had abandoned them. With what seemed like the absence of God's light, their feeling of separation was total and complete.

And, to think, Ego, Mind and Fear had hardly even started. But, that was the way of things.
All that Ego, Mind and Fear had to do was replace awareness of God's love and light with their own thoughts and the whole world changed.

Lucifer crowed, "It was so simple."
God was stupid enough to give all of His creation — Himself in other forms — the same free will to think, choose and feel as He had!

"Didn't He realize His creation could be subverted? That eventually someone would want to dominate the beauty, love, peace and joy of the fabric and change it to suit himself?"

This former heaven on World Earth was so different from heaven. In heaven everything filled the senses with sound and light. On World Earth, there was sound, light and physical touch. It was the physical sense of 'feeling', this sensuality that gave World Earth added excitement and fascination for Lucifer.

He rekindled his knowledge of the workings of heaven and used the energy of sound and light — pure vibration — to change the God-focused vibration of life on World Earth.

Lucifer learned when love was diminished and eventually replaced by fear he could control every mind on World Earth...the mind and the consciousness of all life forms.
Love has no sway over anything other than love.

Indeed, he did become master of World Earth.
Earth angels watched in disbelief as the animals competed viciously to accumulate more than one mate and even fought to their death.

They watched the animals control their territory.
Instead of being a part of all the land, they defined artificial boundaries and began to compete and kill for dominance within their borders.

The actions of their brothers and sisters, the animals, birds, insects and fish confused Earth angels, and they became fearful.

Before long they were fighting off pain and death from a world that had never threatened them before.
They felt forced to kill or be killed.

The original Earth angels were in fact this world's counterpart to heaven's angels. Of course, they did not have wings, but then they were always meant to be the caretakers of God's precious World Earth and had no need for them. They could materialize, etherealize and re-materialize at will.

Apart from flight, Earth angels had all the qualities of heavenly angels. They could communicate with each other with or without words.

They knew when another precious soul was in need, no matter how far away, and could be present — physically or energetically — to help wherever they were needed. The recipients always knew who was helping them.
Missing each other was a concept they did not understand.

They had a full working knowledge of the universe.
With the wisdom of One Spirit dwelling within all life, they knew they were not separate from God, from each other nor from any other form of life.

Just as they were in time with the rhythm of God's heart beating within them as their own heart, they could also see and feel the rhythm of that same heart beating everywhere.

Sunrise and sunset, those magnificent displays of gold, red, orange, pink and purple mirrored their own magnificence. The moon's glow and its mysterious reflections were the luminescence of God's love that lived inside all life. Like the ebb and flow of the oceans, it was a constant reminder of the ebb and flow of the light within them. The light of God pulsed through them with every beat of their heart.

They felt the wind dance around them as they felt their hearts dance. Always aware of God's voice, they heard Him in the wind rustling leaves on the trees, swaying branches, waving grass, living, breathing, caressing the clouds.

Exciting and renewing the atmosphere, carrying the whispers of God's love from place to place. Harmonizing with all the unique calls of life, every sound carried on the wind, filling all space to the delight of World Earth.

Pre-Lucifer, Earth angels walked upon Mother Earth and rejoiced with her as they shared the knowledge of their life's purpose through God's love.

It was their responsibility to nurture and support all of the unique forms of life the Ancients, angels and I AM presence of God had created especially for this planet.

Mother Earth loved God's Earth angels, for they helped her fulfill her role as the foundational support for all life.

LUCIFER'S LIES

She felt them dance, run and walk upon her and the love of God radiated from them into her, warming her heart and soul.

She felt the presence of God through them so fully that it reinforced and amplified the warmth and love she radiated.

She provided the nourishment to grow the seeds, fruits, nuts and vegetables whose consciousness was filled with her love and the light of God. They freely gave of themselves, rejoicing in taking part in the cycle of life upon earth.

Mother Earth also reflected the beauty of God through her ability to use the sun's rays and alchemically turn light within her body into amazing stones of every color.

She studied the light refracting the multitude of colors of the sun's rays and created stones that shone through with a captivating beauty. These stones sparkled from the waters, shone in caves, and gleamed through mountains reflecting God's infinitely creative nature within each facet.

The Earth angels were delighted. They saw themselves reflected in the beauty of the stones.
They felt God's love through them.

The stones loved the Earth angels for they too saw themselves reflected in the eyes before them. They also knew God was looking at them. Subtly connected one to the other, they lived the bliss of freedom for they knew no other way.

There were infinite ways for the Earth angels to help God express Himself in new forms. For millennia they playfully expressed themselves with color, sound, smell, taste and touch.

The flowers and plants were a particular source of joy to create. Untiring and with God's creativity flowing through them, they co-created every expression of beauty they could imagine.

They loved color and were inspired by the depth and variation they saw emanating from each other. They thrilled with the discovery that the exciting colored lights glowing from around their own bodies corresponded to their different thoughts and feelings.

Earth angels glowed intensely when they focused on the essence of God's love flowing through them. Everyone could see all the different colors that lived as God's light radiating from them.

Light emanated from all life on Earth. Because they felt such a sense of peace and joy when they looked upon these colors they decided the sun and rain should join in the fun.

They commanded colored light to appear when water and sunshine met through the atmosphere. Choosing the seven major colors from their own bodies, they called this prismatic delight 'rainbow'.

At the time of Lucifer's arrival, the Earth angels were living lives of contemplation, meditation, creating through

God's inspiration and generally having as much fun on World Earth as possible.

They lived in an abundance of joy.
Peace and harmony was their natural state of being.

They rejoiced at their ever-changing world.
With great enthusiasm they listened to God's words coming from within their hearts. What they heard inspired them to write stories and edify each other with plays and songs and paintings and sculptures.

Their every creation of a new variety of life exhilarated them. The soul's inspiration filled their hearts and minds with joy.

At that point in history, to live and interact with life on World Earth was unquestionably one of the greatest privileges in all of God's creation.

Earth angels loved without exception. They never lost sight of the original precious innocence of the babies and young forms of life which still resided in the mature adult forms.

The Earth angels had so much in common with the Ancients and the heavenly angels.

They had intimate knowledge of the heart as the seat of God's powerful creativity in their own being.
They were aware at all times that their thoughts were God thinking through them.

All their decisions, creativity and inspiration came from this source of consciousness. Understanding how their bodies intelligently interacted with One Spirit was another constant source of enjoyment and cause for appreciation.

They knew they were so much more than just their body, and their souls could manifest consciously anywhere within the fabric.

Unlike heavenly angels, who did not have physical form and could not experience the sensations of touch, Earth angels celebrated the physical senses.

These senses fascinated them and they loved to create new things to feel, touch and see...feathers, fur, their own luminous silky skin, and hair; rock, wood, and vegetation. Hot, cold, warm, soft, hard. They took nothing for granted as they developed all their senses, appreciating each of them as a special gift from God's creativity.

The experience of being on World Earth was one of fun, laughter, peace and joy for all life forms.
Happiness pervaded the very air; it went deep into Mother Earth and every living aspect of the planet.

World Earth was like a magnet to all other forms of life. Every other expression of God, His creations that existed in other parts of His domain, could hardly wait to experience and share in life on World Earth.

Earth angels gladly shared their particular way of expressing God with all who wanted to participate in their world. They knew and felt how special they and their world were and delighted to open themselves to more of God's

LUCIFER'S LIES

wonder in the form of life from other planets.

God welcoming more God!

Mother Earth remained balanced and harmonious because, without exception, Mother Earth and everything upon her maintained clarity and purity of heart, thought, word and deed.

When other forms of life needed to refill their hearts and souls with more love, a visit to World Earth was the preferred choice.
Bathing in this haven, they regenerated their being.

God's love expressed through life on World Earth was a powerful source of pure energy. It was ecstatic in its nature and never failed to bring peace and joy to all who experienced it.

Earth angels felt a great satisfaction in expanding their role as caretakers beyond their planet. Giving of their time and energy with enthusiasm, they were gratified by the transformation of these re-energized souls who returned renewed to enhance their own worlds.

Such was life on World Earth.

Unconditional love is the perfect point of power of One Spirit. It is lived through clear thinking and purity of heart, illuminating all life with light, peace, love and joy.

Pre-Lucifer, all life on World Earth was linked by the energy of this love and communicated with all other life.

The rocks, mountains, oceans and lakes communicated with the Earth angels who communicated with the animals. No one expected Lucifer and his friends to be an exception to the rule.

The new arrivals had everyone excited. The Earth angels remembered the Ancients with great love. They had laughed together and loved each other as they worked to create this new world. The Earth angels again felt the love the Ancients had for them.

They watched with interest as Lucifer and the other fallen angels were awe-struck upon their arrival on World Earth.

They were aware — and a little non-plussed — at how pleased the Ancients were when Lucifer expressed his wishes to stay, stating that he "felt the presence of God's love everywhere."

It never occurred to the Earth angels to wonder why Lucifer was so enamored by God on World Earth.
Hadn't he just come from God's house?
Wasn't he one of God's beloved heavenly angels?
Of course he felt God here!

That should have been a clue that something was amiss. God's love continued to permeate everything all the time.

God is everywhere. God is everything. God is.

Ever so naturally and with trust in their hearts, they accepted and welcomed God's heavenly angels among them.

The Ancients had received instructions.
"Take Lucifer and his band of fallen angels to World Earth. Make sure they settle in. Monitor their transition back to God-focus." Once the Ancients had accomplished that, they were to bring them back.

From Lucifer's behavior, the Ancients expected a long stay on World Earth. Under other circumstances they would have loved to stay for as long as possible.

This world and its Earth angels were most beloved by the Ancients, but God kept them busy as He continued to express Himself in such an expanding and ongoing way through so many diverse systems, galaxies, and universes.

Needless to say, they were astonished at the instantaneous transformation of Lucifer and the others.
Lucifer's rapt features and sincere-sounding words convinced them he had acknowledged the truth once again.

They agreed to allow this band of fallen angels, who they thought were no longer fallen, to stay on World Earth. They were confident World Earth and its beings would only reinforce the wholeness of God's love to these rebellious heavenly angels.

It was with some regret that they themselves no longer had an excuse to stay. The sooner they moved on, the sooner they could continue playing their role as co-creators and caretakers in the multi-dimensionality of God's love, fulfilling their purpose within the fabric of all life.

Lucifer knew full well the Ancients would leave as soon as they could. After all, they were so diligent and devoted to God's cause. One of their jobs was to find God's creations that needed help in realigning themselves back into the fabric.

But this lot had no intention of realigning with God.

God's first expression of Himself from pure energy, pure love, was the Ancients. Next He created a few minor worlds where He experimented with free will. It became apparent that by choosing to lose oneself in physicality a being could become very fragile.

When God sent the Ancients to re-establish these souls back into the harmonious matrix of energy that is the fabric, their power overwhelmed these worlds.

That led God into another exciting expression of creation: the angels. Their appearance alone inspired love in all of His creations thus far.

Heavenly angels played different roles during the course of creation. Although autonomous they always took guidance from God.

The angels had wings of luminescent colors.
Their ethereal radiance represented His love and affected everything in their presence.
God's heavenly angels were pure energy.
Each angel had the gift of music and song.

God was greatly pleased with His angels. He had created them to diffuse the intensity of the Ancients' power so together they could help any part of the fabric in need.

Lucifer and his rebellious followers felt as if they were being 'ordered' to be who they were. To some degree they were right, for God had created the angels for a specific purpose.

The angels remained invisible most of the time as they empowered others with God's love and light. Usually, those in need did not realize who had changed the course of pain into joy.

The majority of God's heavenly angels had not been exposed to World Earth. Their attention had always focused on the adoration and glorification of God.

Angelic music filled the universes with such sweet joy. It created harmonic balance amongst all life, all dimensions, and all universes and beyond. They knew of their brothers and sisters in other dimensions and sensed the glory of God emanating from them.

They loved working with the Ancients.
Both were necessary and loved one another.
And all was well in God's house.
That is, until Lucifer decided to rebel.

All life consists of immortal and indivisible particles.
They are the fundamental building blocks of the universe.
These particles respond to love and were the first
expressions of life to manifest in the 'Big Bang'.
The Ancients were created from these particles.
Everything consists of these particles.

It was in the process of creating the third dimension that
God produced one of His most beloved and exciting species
for expanding more love: the Earth angels.

Through them He more fully experienced the senses of
smell, touch and taste via what God called the human body.

They became co-creators, full participants in an experiment
of grand proportions. They understood how to command the
particles of life through love. Like wingless angels in third
dimensional bodies, their creativity with these particles
seemed limited only by their imaginations.

God invited the Earth angels to create and inspire other
forms of life, infusing divinity through different colors,
shapes, sizes, smells and intelligences.
One could well have asked, "When will it end, this amazing
procreation of exotic, wild and wonderful ideas?"

God infused every particle that makes up the whole of who
we are with His divine love. Every aspect of an Earth angel
was intended to resonate with God at all times through this
sacred love. And it did.

Earth angels were truly inspiring in every aspect of the word.
They dwelled secure in the knowledge that their souls lived

forever within One Spirit's heart and that One Spirit's love — love of itself, love of all life — inspired all thoughts and feelings.

God's spirit is the One Spirit that is all life.

No matter what Lucifer has done or led us to believe, the truth is humans are always connected to and inseparable from God.

God does not separate Himself from Himself.
That which God has created and dwells within, He does not abandon, nor does He punish.
Only humans do that.

LUCIFER'S LIES

Lucifer did an effective job of corrupting life on World Earth. At first there was a lot of work, but once started, Lucifer's brand of magic spread like wildfire with a life of its own.

The Earth angels became extinct because they could not live in a world without God's love.

The devolution of the consciousness of their offspring, now known as the human race, cemented Lucifer's stronghold — the mind.

Once humans had forgotten their hearts were their souls' sacred medium of divine communication, it was but a brief moment before the mind ruled, and the rest is World Earth's tragic history.

In his effort to replace God and achieve total control, Lucifer had to become even trickier still.

He knew that when human corruption reached critical mass, the imbalance and disharmony on World Earth would affect other realms. The fabric would not tolerate or sustain this kind of corruption as life would no longer flow freely from one dimension to another.

Lucifer, understanding the workings of God's worlds, knew the only way his plan could possibly work without detection was to take us only a degree or two from the path of the heart.

What seemed like the heart speaking was really Lucifer and Co. — Ego, Mind and Fear — spreading lies, planting fear and encouraging greed.

In the planning stage he recognized that God dwelled within each tiny cell of these amazing beings, and all life on World Earth. His challenge was to change the balance of things as quickly and efficiently as possible. Once detected it would be nothing short of war between himself and the Ancients.

Lucifer was more than ready to do battle.
He was pleasantly surprised as he had not counted on the humans' resourceful and total dedication to their cause. And now he was their cause!

His plan depended on a simple 'divide and conquer' strategy. His treachery wiped out all memory of who humans really were.
The Earth angels became nothing more than a myth.

Lucifer used his celestial gifts to confuse humans and manipulate their minds. By veiling the heart in darkness and fear he had humans believing that his resonant angelic voice was God's voice.

His seeds of destruction multiplied fruitfully.
They endure to this day.

Humans felt disconnected from God as Lucifer surrounded their hearts with fear and filled their minds with thoughts that they believed were meant to save them from that fear.

The disconnection of the heart from the mind resulted in masses of conflicting emotions.

LUCIFER'S LIES

These thoughts created feelings and, in turn, circumstances that amplified the fear. Humans began to experience anger, resentment, envy and hatred.

Lucifer had effectively divided, separated and finally conquered the human race.

God communicates with humans most directly through the heart. The heart has the capability to direct every indivisible unit of our being. Love is the language the heart uses to direct every fundamental building block of creation.

The Earth angels' cells and neural pathways resonated with the energy of this love and were intricately connected to the love that existed in all life on World Earth. This is the same love that exists throughout the entirety of the fabric.

Just as when the beautiful black snake affected the tree which in turn affected the grass, when Lucifer first clouded the heart with fear, the impact spread until it affected every other part of life on World Earth.

That was when he discovered it was necessary to fill the minds of only a handful of Earth angels at a time and his influence would ripple out into whole communities.

The original humans, that is, the Earth angels, were without suffering or sickness. Confusion and pain were unknown to them. Being the love that they were, their hearts were God's perfect point of power.

The Earth angels knew they were not separate from anything or anyone. They knew there was nowhere and no one who was not of this love, who was not a part of the One Spirit that is God.

That was pre-Lucifer — pre-Ego, Mind and Fear.
Humans have long forgotten who they are.
For millennia, they have been asking, "Who am I?

Why am I here? Where did I come from?"

Having lived in this world for so many lifetimes now, Lucifer has had more than ample opportunity to wipe out all recollection of humanity's original state of being.

He knew it was pointless to attack the heart first.
The heart is God's domain, and until he had lined up his forces to move on the mind he knew it was premature to attack the heart. This had to be a double-pronged attack.

He also understood that without holding the heart under his powerful influence he could never control the Earth angels or their offspring, much less dominate World Earth.

God expressed Himself through the centre of the heart.
So Lucifer, the great tactician, went straight for the heart and the mind at the same time.

Experimenting in different areas of the heart and mind at the same time meant he could maximize their confusion and his amusement.

In order to separate mankind even further from God, Lucifer devised the brilliant and successful campaign to separate men from women.

Together, men and women were a perfect expression of God's love. As the other half of the one soul, man and woman lived in harmonious relationship to each other as mirror images.

Their love for their partners was synergistic and even more

powerful because it was the two of them living the love of God through each other.

Lucifer struggled at first.
Then he remembered the black snake.
He used fear, of course. Like the snake, Lucifer slid out of nowhere and curled a cold blanket of energy filled with darkness and fear over every woman's heart.

He then tightened his malevolent weaving around the heart until the pain was almost too much to bear.

Fear and confusion set in. It was alien to anything woman had ever experienced. These women looked into the eyes of their partners for support but they could not recognize themselves there.

Lucifer had done his job on man also. The image that was reflected back to them was also one of confusion and fear.

Man did not understand these feelings either, as Lucifer had simultaneously wound a dark cloud around man's heart, choking off the pathways of energy from the heart to the mind.

Lucifer's persistence made sure that man and woman were kept busy trying to understand their own brand of fear, let alone each other's.

Lucifer planned a minimal role for women's hearts.
Because he understood the value of heart-based nurturing for the propagation of the human race, he contrived a way to make it appear as a liability of the 'weaker' sex.

Thus, woman still had some feelings via her heart, but it was a continual struggle to feel through the darkness and pain.

Man no longer felt through his heart, as it was insulated by dark clouds of fear. Lucifer insinuated to man that feeling through the heart was weak and only for women. Man resorted almost exclusively to his mind for survival.

By surrounding the heart with thick, impenetrable clouds of fear, it deadened the circuits to and from the heart, resulting in a powerful circuit of energy from the base of his spine straight to his brain and back again.

Man became obsessed by his sexuality.
Having taken the heart out of the picture, Lucifer focused the center of man's physical feelings in his base and sacral energy centers.

This further shattered all life on World Earth.
By separating man from woman and distorting how they related to each other, Lucifer had rewritten the script of their lives to emphasize confusion, fear, pain, jealousy and misunderstanding.

Lucifer and his followers, now openly known as Ego, Mind and Fear, kept revising humans' scripts and, like puppeteers, pulled their strings to perfection.

Through masterful deceit and devilish trickery, Lucifer instigated chaos among all life on this planet.
Humans' lives — unknowingly manipulated by Ego, Mind and Fear — became no more than a game to be played.

Men looked upon women as objects of lust as Lucifer mercilessly pulled their sexual strings hour after hour, day after day.

Women's hearts were further torn in two as their partners no longer looked upon them alone with love, but at all women with lust.

Lucifer had already touched all animal life with this same winning formula. Everywhere on World Earth, life had changed.

Like the animals, man competed with man for the right to be with other men's partners, often fighting and sometimes even to death. All this time, Lucifer fed man ways to gain maximum power over women.

Lucifer's whisperings continue to affect men and women to this day. "Keep them hidden from other men. Destroy woman's ability to enjoy sex so she will not want man the way man wants her. Break woman's heart often enough and she will resign herself to subservience.
You are stronger. You are superior to the weaker sex."
Before long, it all seemed so natural.
Hadn't it always been like this?

Men learned to exploit women with no care for the hearts of their once-beloved partners. And now, as we begin life in the twenty-first century Lucifer laughs uproariously as women exploit men and harden their hearts against them.

More and more, women emulate man's behavior, hurting them as they have been hurt, hardening their hearts in order to compete and conquer.

Ego, Mind and Fear are proud of their accomplishments. They were so subtle in corrupting and diverting the heart from God that, at first, the people did not notice the change.

Human life in its original Earth angel form could not sustain itself without God. They had been a perfect expression of God's will.

Lucifer tricked them by emulating God's energy.
They were deceived into believing they were still hearing their most treasured and beloved God. But after their hearts had been covered, broken and no longer the focus of their being, it became clear that something had gone very wrong.

Earth angels began to fade away, to die out.
In essence, they decided they could not live without love. God had given them free will to live in His world as they chose, but this world had become too hard to even contemplate.

The Earth angels, as Lucifer had first encountered them, became extinct by their own choice. They left their offspring who, under the influence of Ego, Mind and Fear, had made the choice to turn against them, like so many children do today.

These children were adamant that they alone knew what was right and what was wrong. As far as they were concerned their parents, the Earth angels, were clueless,

irrelevant and obsolete. (Does this sound familiar?)
They even talked about a God who did not exist.

The Earth angels could not prove to their children any of what they remembered to be true, as they had long ago lost the ability to live in multiple dimensions. They had lost the use of their human technology. They could no longer heal, prophesy, access divine intelligence or travel the fabric appearing anywhere at will.

Lucifer had done an amazing job undermining the spiritual intelligence of these children who did not even weep when their parents left World Earth. He had begun to manipulate their hearts and minds even before they had been born.

Ego, Mind and Fear adored these children.
They were essential to their cause. What these children did resulted in what we call primitive man.

They were the first generation which Ego, Mind and Fear used to create the world as we know it today.

Lucifer had not anticipated this scenario. His goal was to replace God — to be the God of the world as it existed on his arrival. But, thanks to Ego, Mind and Fear, the light had gone out on World Earth. He had extinguished the light he sought to control. Awareness of God's presence had faded into a shadow of its former self.

On one level Lucifer's plan succeeded beyond his most ambitious expectations. On another level, his success became the problem. He had destroyed the very thing that he loved.

LUCIFER'S LIES

**We cannot possess and control what we love.
Even trying to will alter it.**

In the absence of truth, love and light, his dominion was now over a world of darkness, lies, greed and pain. Mother Earth mourned her Earth angels and cried out in pain.

She tried to shake loose all corrupted life. Volcanoes erupted; she rendered herself apart and swallowed up all she could. The seas swelled under her influence and indiscriminately washed life away.

And Lucifer laughed.

While disappointed that he could no longer play God with the World Earth he used to know, he felt compensated by this awesome display of destruction. Moreover, the willingness of the Earth angels' offspring to accept and love him far exceeded his wildest dreams.

In truth, he had always felt a little discomfort during the conversion process when the devastation of the Earth angels became obvious and unavoidable.
But only a little, mind you.

It was a bit too much like destroying other angels.
And when it would become necessary to go to war with those of his own kind, at least they would know what they were fighting.

But the Earth angels had no idea they were even under threat. Ego, Mind and Fear had rendered their hearts so impotent they had lost the capability to fight back.

What exactly were they to fight? They had an inkling the voices they heard were not from God.

Their souls felt the power shift from heart to mind and were bereft. The Earth angels cried out,
"Why has God abandoned us?"
Was it a joke God had played on His children?

Just the thought that God had turned their world into such a hopeless, smoldering mess was enough to sicken Earth angels' souls.

Lucifer's laughter reverberated through the universe as he realized God Himself was being blamed for his handiwork. "This is too good," Lucifer congratulated himself.
Feeling severed from God, no longer able to function multi-dimensionally, the souls and broken hearts of the original Earth angels suffered miserably in this new world.

They knew no peace and their children, who no longer associated with them, ridiculed them. They were saddened and distraught by Lucifer's corruption of their unborn offspring. These newest souls, still so connected to the One Spirit, were also the easiest for Lucifer's lot to confuse.

Their innocence and eagerness to participate in being an expression of God's love on World Earth meant they were always open to hearing and learning — both from God and their parents — from the moment of conception.

Lucifer wound darkness through the women into the babies and they experienced a loss of light. Fear of the darkness was like a cord around the baby's neck, choking God from their hearts.

It was at this crucial moment, when Fear had done its job that Lucifer, impersonating God, spoke softly to the children. To their minds.

He developed a playground for Mind to romp in.
They played with the unborn babies' minds, telling them their parents did not want them.
They were not worthy of love.

Lucifer told the little girls that their daddies had wanted a boy. And the boys that their mummies had wanted a girl. It is not hard to understand the result of this duplicity.
The babies became confused, then frightened.
What was the point of being born?

A soul in that small physical form is at its most vulnerable. At first, many of these souls could not tolerate the darkness and died before birth. The strongest of these sabotaged souls struggled through the birth process but that too had now become a traumatic experience.

Many died. Fear completely transformed what had been the miracle of birthing new life. Something that had once been filled with love and joy was now overshadowed by pain and death.

Lucifer's lies were so effective that he soon realized he had better back off. He was losing too many of the souls he had counted on dominating.

The shadow Fear cast over the heart was the most productive weapon in the fallen angels' fatal arsenal. The enshrouded heart was all but unknown to these new humans, and it hurt.

That's when Ego and Mind took centre stage.
"We will look after you, beloved child."
"We will protect you from this world, from these people and forces you cannot trust," said Mind.
Ego confirmed this.

These children, Lucifer's first babies, believed that no one knew anything except, of course, themselves.

Their minds, under the tutelage of Ego, Mind and Fear, asserted that only they should have a say in their lives, without regard for wisdom or love, parents or God.
They rejected the truth and became victims of their own choices.

They were the first to lead humanity into the dark ages.
Respect for each other became a thing of the past.
These were truly his people.

Even though this was the most despicable of all his tactics, muddling the minds of our unborn children still reaps his greatest rewards. These children reincarnate lifetime after lifetime and still turn against their parents, against God and against love.

Perhaps Lucifer felt he had gone a bit too far, but the further he pushed, pulled and wove his game throughout World Earth, the more compelled he felt to continue.

LUCIFER'S LIES

His trickery continues to this day. Ego, Fear and Mind still work overtime. There is no limit to their imagination.

In creating that one scenario based on fear he learned from the snake, the tree and the grass that his mind games spread throughout the senses. Like a stone thrown into a pond, the ripple effect of confusion, fear and pain resulted in struggle, frustration and anger.

None of these had been experienced on World Earth before Lucifer's intervention.

What Ego, Mind and Fear focused upon they became.
Their appearance changed over the course of time.
No longer focused upon the light, the ugliness of their thoughts steadily transformed and disfigured their physical manifestation.

This was the inescapable outcome of universal law.
We become what we focus upon.

Earth angels were no more. Those few who remained became Lucifer's pawns to do with as he pleased.

At this stage of Lucifer's reign, it is hard for us to appreciate the shock caused by the fear, pain and confusion of the Earth angels.

These emotions and feelings have become commonplace. In fact, many today talk of accepting these experiences as natural, no doubt in the hope of dissolving at least some of their angst. Many others go so far as to deny the contradictions and agony of living in this world today.

And thus, the legacy of Ego, Mind and Fear still reigns.

Ego, Mind and Fear recognized the importance of gaining control over their new dominion before the Ancients returned.

It was their idea to divide up World Earth and form separate areas of control. They called these divisions countries, then separated the people within the countries from each other by suggesting they could own the land they walked upon.

They swallowed the stories Fear fed them about scarcity. Soon, loss and the need for protection appeared.

They felt the need to create fences, borders, and eventually security systems. People and animals were trained to kill intruders. They invented devices to harm those who dared cross the line.

Together, Ego, Mind and Fear scrambled human communication. Each area developed its own language. Regional dialects further separated people within national borders.

Greed found its deadly way into the world.
Ever since, the world has never been the same.
In this transformed consciousness even differences as natural as various skin colors, cultures, even clothing and hair styles served to precipitate tension and separation.

And Lucifer laughed.
Greed and scarcity combined to cultivate insatiable appetites as humanity confused satiety with satisfaction. Lust and perversion begot more of the same. Most lost their sense of balance and were never satisfied.

Hunger for violence and sensationalism increased until now humans are captivated by movies and media that detail the latest abominations that occur every minute of every day of every year.

And Lucifer's list goes on.

Humanity's reactions became predictable to Lucifer. He felt like he was watching a rerun, day after day, of the only movie in town.

His pride and arrogance led him to believe his own story. He became overconfident in his dominion over the people. To spice up his life, he decided to let humanity spend more time with those who came to talk about God and love.

Remembering the intensity and the gratification of his campaign against Jesus, Lucifer hankered for a comparable challenge.

He wanted something he could sink his teeth into, something worthy to challenge himself, Mind and Fear.

This created the opening the Ancients and the angels had been waiting for. With their help, mankind could achieve the critical mass to precipitate change.

Now we stand at the crossroad. Predicted by prophets from the beginning of recorded history, we are at the inflection point of multiple major cycles that creates an opportunity for change unlike any since the arrival of Lucifer and his lot. These prophecies have foreseen two possible outcomes. Now is the time for us to choose our future, individually and collectively.

One road leads to annihilation yet again, a new beginning through death and destruction. The other leads to transformation, to a new heaven on earth, as we choose peace, love and forgiveness. As we choose God and restore our hearts to their rightful role.

We began to feel the stirrings of hope when the Ancients arrived and, with the angels, began this current cycle of repairing the grid, making the harmony of the fabric inviting and accessible once again.

After World War II, the stage was set for the freedom seekers of the future to break down the structures of the past.

With the threat of nuclear devastation, people began to recognize we are one world. As the focus shifted the anti-war campaigns, free love, flower power and 'greenies' reflected visions of a changing awareness.

People opened themselves to the possibility of living free of the structures, games and boxes of the times that had been accepted as normal.

This was not the challenge Lucifer had in mind, but it would have to do.

As the grid repairs proceeded, the fabric was more accessible, which facilitated shifting consciousness, enabling people to surf the spiritual net once again. Music, art, television, radio and the written word are especially fertile fields for the reception and transmission of inspiration from the multi-dimensionality of the fabric. The Oprah Winfrey Show has exposed hundreds of millions to the practical relevance of spirituality.

In the twenty-first century we feel the impact of many spiritually intelligent beings. Among them, you may recognize His Holiness the fourteenth Dalai Lama, who embodies forgiveness. Mother Theresa demonstrated unconditional love and selfless service to God's people. His Holiness Maharishi Mahesh Yogi teaches enlightenment via meditation to bring peace and happiness to the world.

Their popularity is evidence of the growing hunger to hear and be affected by people that model love, peace and happiness and to watch movies and television and read books incorporating spiritual subjects.

We want to be reminded of who we really are.

This process has given us the opportunity to loosen Lucifer's clutches on our minds. Our hearts, although still feeling fear, are bravely stepping forward despite the darkness, seeking to know the truth once again.

The path that leads us back to heaven on earth is becoming visible. Many are choosing to follow it.

Never in millions of years would Ego, Mind and Fear have believed that God's emissaries would have a meaningful impact upon the children of World Earth and the games they had mastered so well.

They did not count on the people ever wanting change. They allowed us to have our spiritual teachers whilst ever our focus remained steadfastly in the mind.

"Well, you can't win them all," was one of Lucifer's favorite sayings. At last, it applied to him.
His plans began to backfire on him.

TRUTH, LIES AND LOVE

He masterminded the use of fear to keep us in our minds.
He used technology to great advantage in his strategy.

Humanity focused on things outside themselves to manipulate and control their environment and each other. The quest for external power overshadowed awareness of authentic internal power.

Even today, people die of hunger and thirst, whilst humanity spends trillions on weapons.

With the advance of technology from the industrial era to the information age, mankind became able to communicate worldwide in the blink of an eye. No longer were we ignorant of what was happening elsewhere in the world.

As we were exposed to other countries and cultures, a common pattern began to emerge. Tolerance, unseen since the time of the Earth angels, crept back into many lives.

We saw war and wanted peace.
We experienced lies and betrayal and wanted truth.
We felt love and wanted more.

Our awakening to the primacy of love and compassion is changing the course of our world.
Peace and harmony are no longer seen only as distant and idealistic goals. Prerequisites to the continuation of life on this planet, they are once more attainable.

The heart is the light that illuminates the path of peace and harmony.

Despite having been duped into deceiving ourselves, a growing number of people are determined to find peace and to know joy once more.

The whisperings of Ego, Mind and Fear may never cease. But we are no longer babies. We are not without wisdom and awareness. We are not without resources and help. More and more, people feel the need to discern truth from lies, to live love and compassion rather than anger and retribution.

We have listened to the masters speak to us of God, love and truth as the way to freedom. We have known moments of joy. They inspire us to do the right thing — for our world and all life in it.

These messages pierced the cloud of fear surrounding our broken hearts, at last exposing them once again, however briefly, to love and wonder.

In becoming more vulnerable, our hearts become more powerful in what they can accomplish through that vulnerability.

The war rages on within us as it does around us.
As above, so below. As within, so without.

The angels and master energies that live among us, and now the Ancients themselves, bring the sword of truth into our lives. We must allow the sword to cut deep.

Be not afraid if the mind chooses to feel pain as the truth of the games of many lifetimes is revealed.

TRUTH, **LIES** AND LOVE

The heart and soul rejoice.

Now is the time of great change.
What that great change will be is up to us.
No matter what, we can choose to never give up.
We can choose to keep moving from the head to the heart.
It is the longest and most important journey of all.

Everyone is capable of making positive change.
Everyone has the right to know the truth.
The heart reveals the truth.

Never has it been easier for men and women to regain the balance and harmony of humankind's original state of being than now.

If you are reading this, perhaps you are one of the Earth angels who have rejoined the people on World Earth. With the help of the Ancients and the angels, life can again reflect God's love.

It has taken a long time but humanity has made it to this point. The Ancients and angels will not leave Mother Earth and the people of this planet in fear and ignorance ever again.

Never underestimate the power of negativity that still persists in this world. Lucifer has not given up either.

Now is the time to listen carefully to your words.
Ask yourself, do they belong to a child of Lucifer or to a divine child of God?

LUCIFER'S LIES

Consciously develop your emotional, physical and spiritual intelligence. Care for yourself, your loved ones, and all life on World Earth with love and compassion. The animals are also seeking to find their way back into the heart and look to us for love and support.

All living things participate in the oneness of life, in the One Spirit. Will we live that life on World Earth, or will we continue to live lies in Lucifer's lot?

Prayer, meditation, healing and prophesy are invaluable tools of our own human technology.
They are indispensable to living the multi-dimensionality of a spiritually intelligent being.

As we remember who we are, we regain the dignity, grace and compassion of the original Earth angels.

The grid is up!
Multi-dimensional sources of help are continuously available.

You can say "no" to addiction and greed, judgment and gossip. You can say "yes" to your heart's answers to your most important questions.

You have the right to know the real truth, to be honest with yourself about yourself.

It is time to forgive yourself for ever doubting your ability to change.

It is your right to make decisions for the highest and best good of all.

Ego, Mind and Fear are scrambling to regroup.

I do not hear Lucifer laughing now.
Do you?

"Illumination is obtained by rising above one's earthly condition at the command of one's will and realizing one's immortal self which is God within... Awaken God within."

Hazrat Inayat Khan

LOVE:
Jesus Weeps

JESUS WEEPS

It was such a long time ago.
But I still remember it like it was yesterday.
Then again, there are certain memories that endure unto forever, and this is one of them.

I was only a child when it all began. Between five and six, yet I remember the feeling as though it was only a moment ago.

I was playing in the yard, an open space surrounded by our house. Pots of jasmine overflowing with fragrance and charm stood beside majestic palms. This is not how I would have described it as a six-year-old. It is how I see it in my mind at this moment of telling.

As a six-year-old I loved the sand, hot beneath my feet.
I sat amongst the sand running my hands over the earth. They tingled with the pleasure of feeling the life within my hand, touching the life within the sand.
I did not know what I was feeling or why.
But from that day forward I knew.

My mother and father were inside the house. It was midday and the heat was at its most intense hour, in more ways than one.

My mind wandered with my hand across the sand as the sun beat upon it. The sand began to throb beneath my hand. It captivated me...and sent me into a state that could be described as a meditative trance.

As my breathing slowed, my body became calm, no mean feat for one so young when not asleep.
The air around me shimmered as my eyes refocused within the intense light that had formed around me.

Although this light almost blinded me there was a comfort that pervaded my tiny body, almost like lying in the arms of my mother, surrounded by love and adoration...only a million times more so.

A voice spoke to me from within the light.
I was completely aware of this voice speaking to my heart. There was no doubt, no confusion. With the certainty that only the innocence of a child can know and feel, the light relayed the knowledge that would change my life forever.

God, my Father, spoke to me through my heart that day.
"Joshua Ben Joseph, you shall be known as Jesus to this world. Your name means deliverer.

"You are the beloved one of My being who has agreed to remember your Father wholly and without reservation.
You have come to deliver My people back into My heart.
To set them free.

"Jesus, My beloved son, I will speak through you.
I will guide your every step. You will see every being as I see them. From this day forward, your heart will hear My words and feel My feelings."

Images of my life appeared before me.
It was all mapped out, the good and the bad.
I knew I was being tested. Would I turn my back on my heart and choose to live in my mind with the rest of humanity? Or would I embrace the opportunity to step into my destiny and fulfill the imperatives of my heart?

Like a movie, lifetimes played out inside my head. I witnessed the many times I had made the choice to sing this same song to the world and how each time had seemingly failed to reach the hearts of my brothers and sisters.

However, I also witnessed the big picture. There had been many who turned from the negativity of their minds' imaginings, embracing — if only for a moment in history — the heart of God within them.

Without remembering the real truth, this wondrous planet and all life upon it is lost to struggle and doom, bringing sickness to all in one form or another.

TRUTH, LIES AND **LOVE**

The sun's glare paled into nothingness as God's light
illuminated my life — past, present and future.
With the wisdom of the Ancients I gave my heart to
my Father.

Even at such a young age, I knew there would be times of
testing around this decision but I also knew it would be
nothing compared to the regret and loss had I not done so.
This I knew with the entirety of all I had ever been and all
I was to become.

I looked through the luminosity of God's light to see my
mother Mary standing before me.

She too was aware of God's light and felt His overwhelming
love. She was drawn from the house to witness the
awakening of her son through God's word.
Mary held me as I wept tears of joy for what seemed
like hours.

My mother's support and wisdom anchored me in that

current time and place, for a part of me felt as though
I had left this planet.

It was not that a part of me had actually left my body.
It was that I had been reminded of the entirety of my
being. All that I am (which is all that you are) exists
simultaneously on multi-dimensional levels. I became
aware that I was living within all those levels at once.

God's presence enabled me to know both the reality of
these multiple levels and the absolute truth about the
human experience. There is so much more, and we are so
much more, than what we can see, feel and touch, taste
and smell with our mind and physical senses.

From that time forward, I consciously lived wholeness.
That is, every cell of my being remembered God.
Every aspect of my personality was congruent with
my heart and soul.

I knew there was only one existence and all life was a part
of that oneness. Any other way of presenting life was
simply incomplete. Everything was so clear to me,
everything about God, that is. Mankind was another story.

The elation of the experience and the joy of sharing that
experience with my mother (who told me she had been
waiting for this miracle since before my birth) was soon
to be shattered by people's misunderstanding when
confronted by my unwillingness to compromise my
Father's word.

It was impossible for me to share with anyone else what

had just happened. It was so far beyond the normal experience of humanity.

Blessedly, God's revelation came at an age when I could understand the implications for my destiny but I was still too young to step into the public arena as an emissary for Him.

I say blessed for it gave me the time to observe people and their contorted interpretations and strained rationalizations of their beliefs and traditions.

The deviations from life's original experience became clear to me. How was it that people, even children, had come so far from the truth that they no longer acknowledged each other as brother and sister?

I saw the different ways mankind had invented not only to separate themselves from each other but also from God.
My heart began to weep for humanity.

No wonder God felt compelled to reawaken His children to the truth.

I realized the consciousness of mankind had been corrupted to the point where humanity did not even remember it had been given the gift of free will.
How could this have happened?

I did not receive that answer for some time.
It was enough for the moment for me to know my life was to demonstrate the truth once more, and my faith was sufficient for that.

JESUS WEEPS

As a child I had a great deal of fun discovering all the
wondrous things I could accomplish as a being living within
the multi-dimensionality of the fabric of God's existence.
You still call them miracles but they were normal to me.

Sometimes, for fun, I even made things appear or
disappear. I knew what people were thinking and feeling.
I was able to communicate with animals, not only vocally
but also with mental pictures.

The synagogue became my favorite place.
I loved the feeling of God being worshipped.
I found the talk stimulating as it centered around one of
my favorite subjects, my Father.

The synagogue had been like my second home almost since
my birth. As a babe in arms, Mary took me there every day,
wondering when and where God would reveal His intentions
for me. At these times, lying within the arms of my mother
and later, standing with the women and children at the
back of the synagogue, with peace emanating from my
heart, I had my earliest experiences of the light of God
glowing around me.

The women would stand as close as possible to us to share
in this light. Mary just smiled, for unlike the other women,
she knew why they wanted to be close to us.

She too bathed in and shared God's love coming from my
heart and all were touched and drawn to the light.

When my time came to be admitted into the synagogue
as a man at thirteen, the women knew they had lost the

presence of something very special but they were not quite sure what it was. They did not equate the difference in what they felt with my absence.

Mary and Joseph felt the hand of God guiding their lives from the moment they met. Their reverence and devotion to living God's will was an important part of my upbringing and training. Everyday since my birth they spoke to me of God and read to me from the scriptures. I was well-versed and, because of my awakening, had an insider's advantage in understanding God's word.

Often Joseph or Mary, thinking I was lost, would find me with the teachers in the synagogue. I was drawn there like a moth to the light.

These were the happiest moments of my childhood and early adolescence. Many of the rabbis felt the peace and heard the wisdom from within my heart, while others loved my youthful enthusiasm.

Later I understood that I was articulating God's thoughts in our Aramaic tongue. My heart, my mind, my entire being was alight with the love of my Father in the presence of more of His children. I loved it.

There were many among the men who felt as the women had — drawn to the energy of God's love.

There were also many who had totally left behind feeling with their hearts. They had deadened themselves to feeling God, yet they still spoke on his behalf. These men stayed as far away from me as possible.

They resented my very existence.

Division within the synagogue grew as I grew. The older

TRUTH, LIES AND **LOVE**

I became, the more focused I became. My words no longer came from the mouth of a babe but from a man and, to many, the most threatening man they had ever met.

Tension grew within God's house.
I knew this was the foretaste of things to come, not only in the synagogues but wherever I was to go.

The time came for me to go out into the world, away from the mounting conflict and into my next phase of learning. For years, God guided me to different places, far too many to mention here. Each place had a masterful teacher and each held another important lesson to be learnt and lived.

The truth about life, about God, was revealed to me as I traveled throughout the world. Each teacher reminded me in different ways of what I had already known. I understood how, through the fog of being in a body, it was all too easy to forget God's essence living within us.

I knew my body alone could not contain me, and the realm of spirit opened its doors to me.

Living within this world as a multi-dimensional being had many advantages, but by far the most important was the consciousness of living within God's heart at all times.

It is hard for many of you to understand what I am talking about, for you still live in the illusory world that says you are separate from your spirit, which essentially separates you from God.

Of course, this is impossible.

JESUS WEEPS

There is a truth you will all come to know, which is that at no time have you ever been separate from that which created you.

Your Father's love lives within every cell of your being and is the very essence that brings you life. Without this love you would not exist...for this is the love that you are!

You are your Father's love.
His light lives within your being unto eternity.

Many have heard this before but only a handful of people know this to be the real truth.

This is now the greatest challenge upon Earth.
It has been the greatest problem since the devolution from Earth angel to human.

Ignorance of this truth created the perfect scenario for my crucifixion.

TRUTH, LIES AND **LOVE**

You have been drawn into a mist. Although it was not your own creation, you have embraced it fully and live in it without question. You know when the mist thickens around you because you feel pain, negativity, fear and separation.

Be deceived no longer.
Know this: your heart is no longer in control.
Few acknowledge God lives through the heart.
If you did, you would do nothing that brings you shame.
You would live by intuition, thinking and feeling at the same time.

As a spiritually intelligent being, you would use the tools of your birthright: prayer, meditation, healing and prophesy.

Only when the heart leads in complete congruence with the soul can the mind be brought into balance. Your true essence, your soul, cannot hurt another. It cannot lie or make up stories in order to fool others, let alone yourself.

The real you, the being that remembers who you really are, must become fully awake and alert to the mists and illusions created by the mind.

It is time for you to confront and dissipate this cloud that envelops your world. How is it possible to dissolve this cloud of negativity, fear and pain when the cloud is so thick and omnipresent that you assume it is normal?

My beloved children, I also have lived life on Earth and know only too well the ease with which the mind takes control.

Despite the various ways you have been subverted and corrupted, now is the time to become aware of what is right and what is wrong.

To dissolve this cloud that has brought pain, misunderstanding, judgment, separation and lack of compassion and forgiveness, you must first acknowledge there is a problem.

To reclaim your original state of freedom, joy and peace you need to know your life is aberrant.
By accepting this fact, you have taken the first step into reclaiming your life as God intended it to be.

You will never lose your right to choose God and love.
You can always choose to reject the fears that your mind has used to entertain you for lifetimes.
What is your choice?

Giving up the addiction to this form of illusion can be hard, even though the cost is great. The cost is living a distorted view of life in which you feel you have the right to blame others, even God, when life does not deliver your desires or expectations. Ultimately, the cost includes all the pain and sickness, sorrow and greed of your world.

God has given everyone freedom of choice and the right to choose freedom. But you have strayed so far from the truth you no longer know what freedom is.

You have listened to the whisperings of a mind not focused on God, and you have been doing this unaware and afraid for countless lifetimes.

TRUTH, LIES AND **LOVE**

That is why, time and time again, I have come to live among you. You have known me by many names, worshipped me in many different forms and still you have not understood my words.

How can you hear with a mind that has been corrupted by fear?

To hear me you must listen with your heart, open and vulnerable to the pain of the real truth.

The real truth will expose the games you have devised and mastered. Then you will see, feel and comprehend the pain your fantasies have created in both your life and the lives of those who play these games with you.

Are you still asking how humanity got to this point of separation from the truth?

One seed of fear was planted into your hearts.
Those who planted it watered and nourished it and it grew. It grew so fast and so thick that the love within your heart, that part of you that knew God with every breath, was finally smothered.

Your awareness of God faded as thick, dark clouds encircled your heart. With every spurt of growth, fear tightened its grip on your world.

God longs for you to emerge from the fog, to choose to listen to the wisdom of your heart and live from the light once again.

JESUS WEEPS

We, the Ancients, are here to help you.
But will you listen this time?
Do you choose to clear the fog?
Do you choose to honor the awareness of your heart?
Do you know you have nothing to fear?

Your fears and your decisions based on those fears are justified only by the fabrications of your mind.

Heaven rejoices as more and more people once again embrace their heritage. The saying, "Home is where your heart is," could not be more true.

The longest road humanity has to travel now is the path from the head to the heart.

Your choices are clear to us.
Are you ready to do whatever it takes to come home?

God, love, peace and joy live as who you are in your heart. That is why, when you are being the love that you are, when you do the right thing, when you think loving thoughts, you have that strange sensation of being home.

I have wept many lifetimes of sorrow as your games became more and more destructive, as you invented new ways to separate yourself from each other and your hearts.

Destruction, pain and disease have become commonplace. You hear our cries of agony in the thunder of your storms and feel our frustration in the quaking of the earth and still you do not listen.

The destruction you see around you, the conflict between nations, races, religions, genders, is merely reflecting the greatest war of all.

**The greatest war of Earth's history rages on now.
This is the war being waged within you.
It is the war between your heart and your mind.**

This is the same war, the same battle I knew and dealt with when on the Earth, even with God's love flowing through my heart.

The only difference between my life and yours is that I remembered where I came from and who I was.
There was never any doubt in my mind regarding the presence of God within my being.

The real truth is simple and can easily be revealed.
It is up to you to choose to accept it or not.

God lives within you, within the heart of every cell of your being. There is nothing other than the oneness of God's creation, God's energy and God's spirit.

It may appear God exists outside of you when you take on human form. But this is only an illusion because, having lost the use of your spiritual senses, you see and feel others as physically separate and different from yourself.

You are no longer spiritually intelligent.

By giving up this intelligence you have lost the ability to see and feel the energy of love that connects every individual soul within the One Spirit.

Love is the energy, the life force that binds us as one.
This energy is God.

The further from the heart mankind moves, the more uncomfortable people feel using the words love and God. I ask you to know the words God and love as one and the same.

It is time to ask yourself if you are ready to stand up and be counted, to move past the man-made illusions of your lives and perceive reality — to come into present time.

This is the time of God.

God, as love, lives within your heart.
Access to Him begins by simply thinking of Him.
It proceeds by focusing on Him and culminates by feeling Him in your heart.

I know you are ready to embrace a new way of being, to live from your heart, as you lived when you first emerged from a wondrous thought in God's mind.

This is more achievable now than any other time since you first lost sight of God.

TRUTH, LIES AND **LOVE**

In the beginning you did not know fear.
You did not even know that such a word existed.
Now is the time to bravely answer this call to come home,
back into the fabric as a whole and complete thread of life.

**I am calling you forth as of this moment.
I am calling you to leave the confines of your mind and
move fearlessly into your heart.**

Will you come with me now?

If your answer is yes, then together we will succeed in
reuniting humanity and this planet with the truth, with
love, with God.
And this world will weep no more.

My job is to reclaim you for God by helping you to know the
truth so that you will remember who you are and why you
are here.

I lived among you as a man called Jesus in order to fulfill

this mission. It was thought that by the demonstrated action of my life, people would once again remember what they had forgotten.

Success was far from assured.
Negativity, pain and fear had taken root deeply.
Long before my death, I wept within the depths of my heart.

Even with God's love riding the crest of my heart and soul, my mind was still pulled toward your pain and suffering. Your feelings were my feelings.

I felt you because you are who I am. I felt my heart break. I more fully understood and felt the story of mankind. When fear first wound its way into your mind, your immediate feeling was one of loss. You thought you felt God withdraw from your heart. But this was not the truth.

Fear manifested a dark cloud around the heart and clarity was lost in that moment.

The heart panicked, as it still does today, and was desperate to find the way to safety. The mind searched for ways to calm the heart.

"Relax, I will take care of this," it assured the heart as it took control. However, the mind was flying blind and made up stories to keep the heart calm. "We're safe now," the mind conned the heart, comforting it like a parent would a frightened child. The heart believed it.
And the mind loved being in control.

The heart did not fight this overwhelming cloud of fear, as fighting was not even known to it. Meanwhile the mind never looked back. Perpetuating its control became its highest priority.

The heart felt even more cut off from God.

Without God, safety could no longer be taken for granted. The heart, which is the center through which God lives and breathes within you, felt abandoned and bereft.

Fear had won.

The heart, believing it had been abandoned by God, felt helpless. It withdrew and experienced deep depression. Ultimately, it capitulated. Direction no longer came from the creative heart but instead from the administrative mind.

Fear generated a darkness that engulfed your planet like a huge dark blanket. As frightened as the mind was, it was more afraid of losing control.

It began to see fear as a resource it could exploit.

Like a consultant who dramatizes the problems he has been retained to solve and creates new ones to keep employed, the mind manipulates symptoms like a circus juggler and never addresses the cause.

The mind's inability to deal with the cause of fear is the real reason you judge each other. It is why you fight to be right, lie, steal and even kill your brothers and sisters.

JESUS WEEPS

This is what precipitated the cycle of exploitation.

As a race, having forgotten who you are, you became predators, murderers, and rapists, not only of your bodies and your entire being, but of the Earth and all life on it.

The heart's ignorance of what was happening gave the mind carte blanche to frighten you even more.
Except for a few rare people, the totality of love was forgotten. The mind's conspiracy succeeded.

Love, with limited exceptions such as the bond of love between family members, was seen as weakness. Compassion, integrity, the very moral fiber of your race was all but lost.

This was the beginning of the real 'Dark Ages'.
This was the beginning of the rule of the frightened mind that continually fabricated ways to further separate itself from God.

One of the most productive ways to accomplish even greater separation was to blame God for everything that caused pain and suffering. The mind built illusion upon illusion to rationalize the worldview it invented and justified it with still more lies.

Mind games became the narcissism of the mind.

The lies grew. Soon you had God as the one meting out punishment and sending you to hell, abandoning you to the fear of eternal damnation.

You know the most remarkable thing about all this?
God has never changed.

God, whether you believe it or not, has always been and always will be love, the matrix that holds all life together. God still gives you the freedom to choose how and what you think as He did from the beginning. This, too, will never change.

It is only another illusion that you are powerful when operating in the context of the games of the mind.

True power has always and only been exercised and lived through the wisdom of the heart.

Only love weaves the eternal tapestry of all life.

Ultimately, the mind knows it is safe when the heart is in its rightful role as the decision maker, in concert with the soul and in consultation with God and His emissaries.

Only when each aspect plays its God-given role can you exercise true power.

JESUS WEEPS

The heavenly realm is working double time at this precarious moment in history to provide you with all the resources and information you need.

It presents countless ways to empower you to choose to be vulnerable enough to regain your original, authentic God-given power. He has been sending His angels and emissaries to inspire you to come out of the darkness that is fear and back into the light of love.

In aligning yourself with love, you are filled with all that is God. You walk in the light and all becomes clear.

What started as a mist of fear and confusion around the heart has become a raging storm of lies and delusions within the head.

Lifetime after lifetime accumulating memories of pain and disappointment has brought you, individually and collectively, to this point of crisis.

TRUTH, LIES AND **LOVE**

The widespread recognition of the need for a brave heart in this sense has only begun since this newest wave of awakening started in the second half of the twentieth century.

At last, God's words are making sense to you again. You are willing not only to listen, but to feel love once more. Those increasingly pain-filled lives have reached the point of saturation.

Not knowing where to turn next for help, the mind turned its attention to the New Age.

The New Age was a hook we used to pull you back toward God — to help you begin to see how far from love your race and your world had come.

The focus of the New Age was intended to be on God and the real truth. Not surprisingly, the mind subverted this. Its tactic of diversion succeeded. Focus shifted.
Under the guise of the New Age, old fashioned exploitation of each other's trust began again.

People became self-proclaimed experts in their minds' fields and the separation that existed before the New Age gained a new partner in crime. You had to become masters of everything. Crystals, healing, meditation, channeling and the list goes on. Like any tool, you can put them to positive or negative use.

New Age tools were the bait on the end of our hook.
But as the original God connection was lost, so aspects of the New Age became just other aspects of the Old Age.

The mind abandoned the perennial wisdom that always returns the heart to God and love.
It refocused attention on what it could control.

To its great relief, the mind succeeded in commercializing the tools of the New Age. So long as the focus on the heart had been subverted, the mind was happy. The narcissistic self-absorption of New Age mind games brilliantly served the mind's agenda.

Remembering God and your relationship with Him could very well mean abandoning the games of the mind and living from the heart.

The mind had to work hard and fast once the heart tasted love. To the mind's dismay, it could not convince the heart it had not felt the love it had experienced.

However, the mind found a way to undermine the impact of these feelings.

It assured those who had taken the bait that they were better than those who had not — what they had learnt and the love they felt set them apart from those who did not even understand what they were talking about.

The mind injected separation into our efforts to empower you to see and understand the possibility of reuniting your minds, hearts and souls.

People believed their system had given them the inside track on love and the exclusive franchise on the truth.

If you were not interested in the New Age (or in agreement with their theology, whatever it happened to be), then you were obviously less loving, not to mention less enlightened, than they were.

It became another scenario of them and us.
This sounds familiar, doesn't it?
And of course this is not the truth.

It is the same illusion propagated by all of the intolerant religions of the world, but in contemporary packaging. (This is similar to what happened around what I said and did during my life, and even more so after my death.)

Fortunately, our efforts did not lose out entirely to the mind. There were those who swallowed the bait 'hook, line and sinker' and they knew they were 'home' again, safe once more within God's heart.

The heart's bravery nudged its way into the minds of those people who had taken the bait. Others, who could not by-pass the mind and grasp how to live with passion from the heart, nonetheless adopted a new way of thinking that still encourages them on the path from the head to the heart.

And for that the whole exercise was worth the effort. Indeed, even a mere handful can affect the world.

The results included feelings that helped spread goodwill and love. For the first time in eons, humanity began to work together using the tools of your own human technology, including powerful demonstrations of coordinated community meditation and internet-facilitated worldwide prayer.

The restoration of your spiritual intelligence as a race has commenced.

You are receiving important messages.
The understanding of the necessity to reconnect to the love hidden within the heart is taking root.

Total health and joy are your natural birthright from God.
You wander through life as though this were a myth.
Do you really believe the perfection that is God would intend to create anything other than perfection?
Sounds crazy, doesn't it?

However, corruption comes easily to minds that have spent countless lifetimes using their free will to only play their games.

These games are frightening. The main aim of the game is to keep you out of the heart. The results of the game are seen in how effectively you scare yourself into sickness and unhappiness.

When the truth is revealed, there is no denying it.
Still, the mind turns a blind eye as the addiction to the intoxicating game draws you back into the powerful magnetic field of fear.

Fear has captivated, entranced and entertained mankind for so long that helping you accurately perceive it has become God's greatest challenge.

Be assured, no challenge is too great.
Our work will continue until every soul remembers the truth, embraces the truth, and courageously lives through the heart no matter how broken and fearful it may be.

As you recognize these words to be from love, supporting and nurturing you to regain your original authentic power, so the seed of love planted by God will sprout and bloom.

JESUS WEEPS

Feel that place deep within your heart that already knows these things. Working together proactively, we can best guide you home — to reality, into truth, back to love.

TRUTH, LIES AND **LOVE**

On the day I was conceived, the seed of Christ consciousness from God's heart that was planted in my being was again planted deep within you. I say deep, because God felt it necessary to hide this precious gift so that your minds would not destroy it.

The seed was centered in your heart. The heart was so clouded by pain, sorrow and fear you hardly knew it existed.

We love this story making the rounds in the angelic realm.

Thinking out loud, God was trying to make up His mind about where to place the seeds of love, of Christ consciousness, so the minds of mankind would not find them.

"I can't very well place them on the moon. The Americans will find a way to go there and they will find them.
I know. I can put them on top of the tallest mountain in the world. No, that won't work.
The English will climb it and they will find them.

"What if I was to place them at the bottom of the deepest part of the ocean? No, that won't work either.
The Russians are sure to go there.

"I've got it! I know exactly where to plant the seeds of love where mankind will never think to look.
I will place the seeds of love, of Christ consciousness, deep within their hearts."

My life and that seed are the catalyst for you to discover

for yourself that all that I am lives within you, too.

Once you became entrenched within your games, it became necessary to hide the seeds from view to ensure their survival until you made the choice to live from your heart.

No matter how God tried to love you back to Him, your fearful minds ran from Him and His emissaries.

In a jigsaw puzzle there is a big picture.
You are crucial figures within that picture.
For the picture to be complete you must be whole and live truth.

No matter how crucial a piece you are to the picture,
I would never force you back into it.
All I could do was love you.
In loving you, my life demonstrated God's love.

It should have been so easy, but instead I found myself bombarded by the consciousness of the people of Earth. Every day I had to fight for my sanity, my heart and soul.

The tests never stopped.

They were not the tests you might imagine. The group mind and fearful hearts were my constant challenge.

I had nothing to do other than to love you.
But love has no command over anything that is not love.

By that time, humanity had hidden love so deeply within them that I heard only their minds.

TRUTH, LIES AND **LOVE**

The heart had to struggle to be heard at all.
Your thoughts went straight into my heart.
My heart felt wounded by your judgments.
I grieved because of the continual darkness of your thick clouds of fear and illusion.

A group of souls who agreed to support my life on Earth were an important and integral part of my mission.

You know some of these men and women as my disciples.
Moses and Elijah also played critical roles and a host of angels, including the Archangel Michael, were my constant companions.

I could not have endured your pain and distress without the constant help of God, His emissaries and His angels.
With their love and support, it was easier to walk with you.

I wept less often for the lies that hid the truth and caused you so much grief.

During the course of my life, I lived and worked among other illuminated souls. I spent precious time with these masters until it was time for me to step out into the public role God had planned for me.

These people exist within each time in your history.
Like Gandhi, like Francis of Assisi, they are the light that helps balance the darkness.
Their presence provides a positive demonstration of how life can be when lived from the heart.

At this time, it is not only the illuminated ones who support the fabric of life. Many people are dedicating their lives to knowing God, to living love and diligently staying awake and alert to the influences that so easily take our focus from the truth.

I am alive and well, supporting you through the trials and tests your minds weave into your daily lives. The seed my Father planted within you still exists. Not only does it exist, but it is now pushing its way to the surface.

You feel it in those divinely inspired moments when looking at a sunset or into the eyes of a baby or beloved animal. The heart feels joy and the mind loses focus for just a moment, and you are in awe of nature — of what you see and what you feel.

What you feel is that seed bursting forth, blooming in that moment inside your heart. With anticipation this tiny yet powerful seed feels the promise of life.
The light within you ignites and you glow.
This is the radiance of love.

How many times have you seen someone who has 'fallen' in love? Do you remember the glow, the radiance emanating from them, and how everyone envied their happiness?
You have probably experienced this love and envy yourself.

True love is unconditional.

No matter what your partner does or says, you do not judge him or her, or separate yourself from them.
The imperfections you perceive in your partner do not concern you.

TRUTH, LIES AND **LOVE**

The heart loves with clarity and purity.
It knows that all life is love; with purity it knows it is that love. You have always known the truth.
This is the reason why there is so much fear in your lives.
To live the truth scares you as nothing else.

In order to protect yourself from yourself, you maintain the illusory mist surrounding your heart and allow your mind to fragmentize you into as many boxes as it wishes to construct. These boxes are the games you play to keep yourself small.

A life lived in the heart is alive, radiant and expansive.

Living in boxes built of the mind's illusory beliefs
is contracted, fearful and filled with death.
These are what you call mind games!

You have felt this and experienced the fruits of your games in every dimension in all of your lives.
My death was the fruit of the games played out by almost every faction of my time.

Can you imagine the tears God wept the day I was crucified? The Ancients and all God's emissaries and angels wept, too. The sky, the wind, the rain, thunder and lightning, even the Earth trembled that day, all expressing frustration and agony at mankind's ignorance.

My physical death was not the source of frustration.
All life is ongoing whether it is in spirit or in a body.
The love that you are cannot die. That would be the same as saying the love that is God would cease to exist.

JESUS WEEPS

I was as close to God and to you after death as during my lifetime with you. The real tragedy and source of sorrow, once again, was the rejection and denial of the heart. The mind still reigned supreme. It had won the game which it saw as a fight for its very life.

To let me live was to let love live. And that meant the heart would regain its rightful role of leadership.

My existence shattered all the boxes of different beliefs that the mind had crafted with such care, and had meticulously handed down, generation after generation.

Most people grew up learning hatred and fear of those who were different from them. Because these emotions supported the mind's agenda, emphasizing and criticizing the differences between each of you became one of the main games in your collection.

Separation from your heart was paramount to keeping the mind securely in control. Separating one from another was a valuable tool that kept other hearts out of the picture. Creativity in devising, exaggerating, and experiencing differences has become nothing less than masterful.

Man has dominated woman since the original break from God's love. Now woman takes on man's roles and fights fire with fire.

Woman has learnt all too well from man, and now many women have become sexual predators.

Even today, there are both men and women who still

believe it is natural, even acceptable, for people to suffer betrayal and injustice at the hands of the opposite sex.

Have you noticed this pattern of behavior within your societies, within the different countries and throughout the different religions?

Both women and men were burned at the stake for being healers. Were women also burned at the stake because of the myriad lusts of man?

Burning and destroying what you cannot have, what you cannot control in yourself and others still happens today. By building himself up, whether through his religious beliefs or his so-called masculine superiority, man has kept woman in her place. Right inside the smallest box he could devise and there she sat, believing this was her place and her lot in life.

This is changing. Part of the world has finally awakened and begun to say, "This is wrong. This is not acceptable!"

There was little I could do about this in my time.
However, I brought my mother, my female cousins and Mary Magdalene into my inner circle as equals.
They, too, were my disciples.

The twelve men chosen by my Father were at first nonplussed and confused. How could I allow women into our meetings and religious discussions? This was a new concept for them and pushed them beyond what their strict upbringing considered right and proper.

I love you all equally and I explained God loves you all equally.

Do not separate yourself one from the other.
Your Father created within each of you the perfect balance, the other half of the coin so to speak.
Woman is the counterbalance to man and vice versa.

Know that within each of you there are both feminine and masculine qualities.

I use the word quality in the true sense of the word, for you are truly an amazing fullness of God's love that has infinite quality.

You are complementary to each other and were created as equals in God's eyes.
This worked perfectly until you began to forget God.

My Father was replaced by a pseudo god.
Many other gods sprang up throughout your world.
This, too, suited the mind as every new god, like every separation between people, served the plan to subjugate the heart. It is this domination of the heart that we have been striving to erase from this world.

You have made your choices. You have chosen to live using your mind as the primary source of guidance.
Logic has become paramount.

What you are just beginning to understand is that logic does not always reveal the truth. Logic is just a tool in the hands of the mind who is the craftsman using it.

When logic serves the mind's agenda of control and separation, it cannot be trusted. When the context or the assumptions and the data are illusory, logic yields only illusory answers.

The reason you cannot trust logic and the workings of the mind is that the mind has been polluted by fear.
Fear is an enigma.

It can take the form of jealousy, anger, manipulation, lies and fantasies. Fear is behind greed, need, justification and denial.

Loneliness, unhappiness and sickness are just a few of the symptoms of fear-based thinking. Domination, exploitation, gossip, hatred, slavery, mental instability, bigotry, rape and murder are other symptoms.
This is what you learn from living in your societies.

Every society feeds the insatiable needs of the mind.
No matter what society you point out, even the most religious, you will find fear dominating the human condition.

Many of you tell yourselves this cannot be true.
If this were not true, there would be no need for my presence among you. My heart would not break for you and my eyes would no longer weep.

God will forever rejoice when you are brave enough to acknowledge that you no longer live in your heart. That you have rejected God's care.

It is not up to God to stop your untimely deaths or the horrors you inflict upon each other and yourselves.
These are the results of your choices, the harvest of fear.

Century after century, I have heard many say,
"Why does God allow such pain and sorrow?"
This is another 'logical' delusion that serves the mind's goal.

The more we can blame God for our current conditions, the easier it is to keep the heart in the dark.
I cannot emphasize enough, God lives within the heart.

This is the seat of His existence within your physical, energetic, bio-electric form. His love lives within the heart of every cell that makes up your human body.

Take off the blinders of the limited mind and introduce yourself to the huge, magnificent and infinite world of the heart and soul.

This is my way of saying, "Let the heart do your thinking." While there would be no need for my presence among you if you chose not to live in fear, that does not mean I would no longer be a part of your lives.

Know this: I live deep within your hearts.
The seed of love that I am is the same seed of love that you are. I could never leave you. I love you with all that I am, which is all that God is. We are each a spark of life constantly changing form. God's love is our essence.
We exist through His grace.

TRUTH, LIES AND **LOVE**

We began as pure spirit, a spark of love from the heart of God. We are a part of the whole of all that is and all that ever will be.

God, of course, is all heart. He is pure love. And that love can be seen and felt as brilliant and perfect light.
The presence of this light catalyzed us into our current body. It is this light, and the love that is this light, that will sooner or later dissolve all negativity from your lives.

To do this you must first commit to becoming whole again. And how can you do this when you have forgotten the meaning of wholeness?

Wholeness cannot exist without truth.

This is why I speak to you now.
You are more than ready to hear the truth.
You are babies no longer. You are not without wisdom.
You are ready to begin the adventure that will take you back into your hearts, back to wholeness.

Courageously listen to every word you speak and examine every reaction you have to everything in your lives.
Be awake. Be aware.

When you feel negativity, fear or pain, know that you have caught yourself in one of your games.

You have hooked yourself back into old habits, old and outmoded ways of being. This is an easy and reliable marker for you to use.

In living by this simple statement, you will be on your way
to clearing the mists of illusion from your hearts.

Take total responsibility for everything you do and say.
Ask yourself, "Am I feeling negativity, fear or pain?"
If so ask, "What have I just said or done? How do I need
to change?"

When you are prepared to be accountable for being the
creator, director, producer and star of your own life you
will at last be able to discover the decisions you have made
that repeat the same patterns you have lived time after
time, lifetime after lifetime.

These are the destructive patterns you see and read about
in the news night after night. They are the same; just the
players have changed.

The stage and the setting, the lighting, producers and
direction may have changed but the underlying dynamics
and causes remain the same.

And people react the same way to these events.
You have become numb to them. Unless you are directly
affected in some way, you have the ability to watch and
listen to the madness of this world and react as though it
were just another Hollywood movie.
And you do not think this is abnormal. Wake up!

You were not created to live in misery and pain.
Your life is intended to be a celebration of God's love.
You are here to experience the wonders, fun and joy,
friendship and love of God through a physical body.

TRUTH, LIES AND **LOVE**

It has always been your God-given right to choose these experiences. Look closely at your choices now.
Are you thinking, "If I really had a choice, why would I have chosen this body or these events in my life?"

You can only say that if you are not prepared to own up to what you have created by your own choices, lifetime after lifetime. Many of the choices and decisions made in previous lifetimes still run the show and drive the games in your life at this very moment.

You have forgotten God.
God does not hate or feel jealousy.
God does not murder, accidentally or otherwise.

Love exists. It gives of itself with no expectations.
Love has no boundaries. It cannot be contained within the tiny boxes of the mind's invention.

You have become your own pawn in a game called life, and you are nowhere near winning in the truth-stakes.

You will never know the truth whilst you deny the need to change. Telling yourself, "everything is fine," reinforces your hearts shutdown, both emotionally and physically.

You can continue to cover your body in protective layers of fat, but the illusion of being nurtured by the food and protected by the fat is just another way to hurry you out of your body and into your next life.

Choices, like acceptance of an abusive relationship without telling the truth about how you feel, and not taking action to make necessary changes, eat away at you. Then you wonder, "Why me?" when you are diagnosed with cancer.

Your body is the mirror of your thoughts.
It will always truthfully reflect what you have been thinking, feeling and saying.

Unfortunately, the primary way it can get your attention these days is through pain and disease.
What you think, the choices you make and how truthful you are in every moment of your life determine whether you will succeed, fail — or even survive — in this deadly game that has become your life.

It is time to go beyond the game.

You can do it.

Are you ready to stop living a life of pain and misery, dotted with the few odd moments of what could be called happiness?

If you experience only one second of true joy and feel the bliss of that one second, you will know it is possible and you can work toward that state of being as your normal state of existence.

Not only is it possible to live in that state, not only is it preferable, but it is more important than anything else you could do.

Your heart is your true source of power and wisdom.

Although you have allowed the heart to remain covered by the mists of illusion and allowed the mind to take over the role of decision-maker, this does not make the mind capable of running your life.

You have given your mind authority over everything, which means you live from a place where control is the highest priority.

You are so much more than your mind.
Your heart and its awareness is who you really are.

Through the heart and its awareness, life is lived with compassion, integrity and love. All decisions made from the heart will manifest that love.

Even if it does not feel like it, the heart is always at work within you. Your heart is aware of what your immediate world is transmitting. It is aware of everything transmitted to you from anywhere in the universe.

It is via the heart and its awareness that you can best direct your thoughts and develop your consciousness.

The problems of your world originated when you transferred the leadership role of heart and its awareness to the mind.

The mind, which was never designed to have the wisdom of the heart, has taken control. It has led you to believe that without its leadership your life and indeed the entire world would be in a far worse state. The mind tells you it alone can solve your problems and protect your safety.

Know this: The mind cannot do this. Moreover, even if it could, it would not, for that would make its role redundant. In its current role the mind thrives on problems and threats. In fact, if there are not enough problems, it creates them.

The root and greatest cause of pain grew and took hold when you denied the heart as the source of wisdom, love and compassion. This, beloved one, amounts not only to the denial of the heart but the denial of God.

TRUTH, LIES AND **LOVE**

You constantly receive information through the energy matrix of all life. It comes through your emotions, dreams, intuition, and the body and you either acknowledge it, interpret it or block it according to your current set of beliefs.

You could allow the heart and its awareness to decipher everything around you and then direct the mind to live consciously with the use of this information. Instead, your mind, with its grand games, keeps you in the dark. Its lies deny the truth of what life truly is and could be.

Life has become a playground founded in fear.

From the fear of the mind not directed by the heart, greed has run rampant through each of you.

Fear, often in the guise of insufficiency, motivates humanity to lie, rob, cheat, and even kill to get what it wants. Brother turns against brother, son against father, partner against partner, neighbor against neighbor and so it goes, on and on.

Thoughts of fear and thoughts from fear have made this world believe in scarcity. The fear of not having enough breeds the disease called greed — a win/lose game that guarantees scarcity for most and imbalance for all.

The heart knows nothing of scarcity; it lives from within the abundance of God's love.

Is it not time to exercise your right to return control of your life back to your heart? To live the light that you are? God's love and His light continue to work with you even when you are oblivious to it. Denial does not stop the truth from existing. No matter how consistently your mind covers it up, the truth remains the truth.

You are never alone in this universe.
God lives within you. And you, beloved, are immortal.
The seed of love that is who I am lives within you.
Angels and the Earth itself will always provide support and guidance when you intend to receive it.

There is a way to experiment and know the truth of my words but that requires you to no longer allow your mind to run your life.

The mind is a wonderful servant of the heart.
It, and you, will find peace and balance only after you take back your right to live from the heart.

Dispel the mists surrounding the heart by saying "no" to fear. This has always been and always will be your choice to make. This is freedom; use it wisely.

No matter what circumstances you are in, you always have the right to choose your thoughts.

Why continue to allow the mind to choose for you?
Our world of chaos and fear is living proof of the disastrous state the mind would have you live in for the sake of its keeping control.

The choice is clear.

TRUTH, LIES AND **LOVE**

Life is lived from one of two places: LOVE or FEAR.

Love is the constant you use to find the grace to forgive, to experience compassion, to allow others to have their say and to stay balanced regardless of what is happening around you.

Fear denies the heart which results in the lack of trust in the order of all life. Stubborn insistence on revenge prevails only when we forget love heals all situations.

To acknowledge your heart as the primary guiding force in your life is a critical first step back into the heart; only then can you free yourself from fear and judgment.

This game with which you have entertained yourself for so long — using fear and the horrors of your world via movies, media and, yes, reality — can end whenever you choose.

Considering how difficult it appears to be for you to relinquish the mind's control, this game of scaring yourself to death must please you. If you refuse to change the rules and it is fear you really want, then why not face the fear of knowing the real truth?

You would have the opportunity to be entertained on a grand scale, for the mind is terrified at the prospect of losing control. Not only would this be fearful, but no doubt you would have a huge fight on your hands.

Your life is constantly going in the direction of your love and focus. Therefore, what you love and focus on directly influences everything you feel, think and become.
If you think you need another game to replace the one you know and love, why not go beyond the game and begin again?

Do not expect the source of the problem to be its solution. It will take nothing less than a complete change for you to understand you have loved fear and the by-products of a fear-based belief system. If not, you would have chosen another way.

Have you forgotten how powerful you are?
Have you forgotten that by your thoughts so has your life become what it is today?

Jumping out of 'judgment' and into another of the current theories, such as 'There is no right or wrong', will create just as much havoc, chaos and destruction.
This is another of the illusions that the mind uses to rationalize not accepting responsibility for your actions, words and thoughts.

TRUTH, LIES AND **LOVE**

You have had many lifetimes to perfect your games and become masters of denial.
Everyone has had the opportunity to experience the horror of loving fear.

This does not mean it is right in the eyes of your Father. God does not condone this, but weeps as you continue to hurt yourself and each other. He has sent so many messengers of the truth to show you right from wrong. But the mind has such deep-rooted power that you have chosen to kill many and reject all.

To justify its illusions the mind lies — with devastating results. The darkness around your heart grows as false hope feeds it with even more lies.

The greatest fear you face is walking into your heart.

It is time to challenge the darkness, to acknowledge and face down the fears and confront the lies. Once you have done this and, make no mistake, that journey into the unknown realms of the heart has begun, you will come face to face with what you have always known.

You turned away from the loving wisdom of your heart to live from the mind's compulsion to control. This has led to all the ills of this world. They are directly related to your choices, not God's.

God is not the scapegoat He has been made out to be. God supports, loves and honors you. He does not destroy you and has no need to punish you. (You already do a good enough job of punishing yourself and others.)

There is no one to blame for anything your life dishes up
to you. Accept responsibility. Be accountable.

**By your thoughts and ideas and especially by your fears,
your life unfolds into the sum total of the choices you
have made.**

Take responsibility for the way your world works now.
Be accountable to your heart for your choices and for
your evolution back into God consciousness. Wake up.
Conditions have never been so conducive to positive change.

More and more people have an inkling of what is possible for
them and their world. The trick is to stay focused on the
heart, on God, at all times; otherwise the mind in its
desperation to stay dominant will continue to deceive you
again and again.

I have watched and supported the heart's attempts to listen
to those of us who come to be of service to humanity.
We show you by our love the goodness of the heart.
You immediately feel the love and the light.
Sometimes it is like a burning arrow through your minds and
then, of course, after that the fear sets in again.

The sword of truth must cut deep.

When lies are exposed by truth, the mind reacts with pain.

On hearing the truth, the mind persuades you your heart is
broken once more. Another opportunity lost...Yet this is not
entirely true, for every encounter you have with truth and
love acts cumulatively.

Despite the mind's remarkable diligence the heart is always alive, ready and waiting. As God will never give up on you, so, too, the heart will never give up its work either.

God and the heart are one and the same.

Many people began to understand this once they had walked with me. They described my heart as the sacred heart. Do you know why?
When they were in my presence, they knew the real truth.

The heart's vibration, when aligned consciously to God, emanates waves of energy that can entrain other hearts to God. In the same way, when fear fills the mind and enshadows the heart, it can catalyze fear in others.

The energy of love in my human state had higher amplitude with a fuller range of frequencies than most. As a result many people felt lightheaded, even euphoric, around the powerful vibration of these frequencies of my body, heart and soul.

Love is the power that heals and performs what you call creative miracles, like those recorded in the Bible.

Faith in the mystery of God is needed today.
The mind cannot explain God. When the mind cannot explain something, it fabricates an explanation that serves its agenda or it dismisses it as unimportant. Other times it entertains itself with the subject, such as the scientists' and philosophers' race to prove or disprove the existence of God.

Scientists and physicists worldwide are coming to the same place. They are finally discovering the secrets of the working of the universes. This information is not complete yet. Soon they will discover the final and crucial indivisible units of life.

These units are the irreducible, fundamental building blocks of existence. These units are the essence of all life. Love and the spirit of God compose the matrix. They exist unto forever, as they are the original units generated by love. The love contained within them cannot be lost. Their energy is directly from God.

These irreducible units of life form the basis of all life everywhere.
They are an expression of the infinity that is God.
Love directly influences these minute, indivisible particles.

It was my love and its command of these units that permeated the atmosphere around me. All in the vicinity who resonated with that love were healed.

No one denied the existence of love, nor the power and wisdom of the heart whilst affected by my love.

This is because their irreducible units of life responded as they gave the right of decision back to the heart.

The mists of the heart cleared enough to reveal a light so welcoming, supportive and nurturing that they knew they were safe — they knew they were home.
Many collapsed into tears of joy.

TRUTH, LIES AND **LOVE**

A joy incomprehensible to the mind.
This is the joy of your Father's love.
And by this joy many were healed.
The more people were able to open their hearts and keep fear at bay, the greater the healing.

This is how I raised Lazarus from the dead.
He had passed into complete oneness with God on his death.

His heart, his entire being was love.
All I had to do was call on the love of his irreducible units of life to reunite his soul and body for Lazarus to be complete in his human form once again.

This is not magic and miracles. Yet, in another sense, you could call all of God's plan and creation just that.
As expressions of awe and wonder, 'magical' and 'miraculous' are appropriate adjectives for my Father's handiwork.

Love is constructive. Fear is destructive.
Turn and embrace the love that you are and you, too, will shed tears of joy from experiencing God's infinite love.

It is more love than you have thought possible for any human to experience. This was your true, original, and most honest state of being. It can be again.

This is also when you will need all the faith you can muster.
At the very moment the euphoria of love takes your senses reeling, the mind will kick into action.

"How can I stop this feeling? What is it? This cannot be good!

Why me? What will everyone think when I tell them what has happened? Does this make me a freak? Or better, more advanced than others?"

Round and round, the merry-go-round of your thoughts will continue to race. The mind will work overtime to find ways to separate you from this love. Your mind warns that your loved ones will ostracize you if you are different.
"Stop all this God nonsense, now!"

Or, "OK," the patronizing mind might say, "you can have these moments if you insist, but don't think you are going to live like this. It's much too unsafe. It's not normal."

Eventually, the mind's persuasion wins the day.
It has reduced your real experience into something that fits neatly into a box. By choosing to listen to and go along with the fear, you lose part of the light.

Perhaps now you can better understand the reaction of many of the people I had healed and loved when it came time for my judgment.

Yes, their lives had been changed, some permanently, some only briefly. Fear and lies flipped most of them back into their normal state of being.

As the choice to surrender to the consensus reality of their neighbors and culture had them cry out for my death, their hearts cried out with anguish and loss. Not one of them understood what they were doing. They thought they were saving themselves from the unknown, from the fearful, troublemaking philosophies of a traveling rebel.

Of course, there were also many people who, once catapulted into the heart and the light of God, would not consider the desolation of relinquishing God's love.

There was no denial of who I am to these precious souls. Even though the mind tried its best to intervene, for them it had truly had its last days of control.

For them to live the message I had delivered from our Father took a willingness and readiness of the whole being to find and live a radically different life. It demanded bravery of the heart and the mind. A handful of these courageous souls remained uncorrupted. They were in command of their thoughts as they looked fear in the face with their brave hearts.

These were the ones who told the stories to everyone they met. As the seed of love planted within their hearts grew stronger year after year, these were the people others could relate to. The light within them was contagious as they transmitted the word of God.

People will always be touched and feel the goodness and healing effects of a heart that remembers God, for that is a heart that is awake.
(All hearts love; most are asleep.)

Even after I had completed that lifetime, I continued to have an enormous energetic impact on those open to my love. That has never ceased. It never will.

Many people felt the love of God through my disciples, including my mother Mary and Mary Magdalene.

They knew the love that I am could not leave them.
They allowed that love to guide them into awakening
others' hearts.

Despite the real threats from even mentioning my name,
more and more people cleared the clouds of fear from
their lives.

Although we modeled the truth of love as the way to
happiness, not enough people participated in it to
overcome the mind's stronghold of fear, which continued
to strengthen and grow.

The greater the progress love made in the heart's
emergence from fear, the harder the mass mind worked
to overthrow this new threat to its power.

Remember, the mind seeks control; its domination is
founded on fear-based thinking. The mind has created
amazingly effective games of deception, separation, and
denial in order to hide the truth.

The mind is convinced it must create boxes to keep you
under its dominion. Using fear and greed, it creates
structures to serve its agenda.

**Love, and the wisdom and awareness of your heart, is
who you are.**

This is the source of the guiding light which alone can bring
your thoughts, your being and your life into balance.
Your goal, as a wise, compassionate child of God is to live
in wholeness, with all aspects of your being in balance.

If you choose the games of the mind, which are the lies your thoughts generate to protect you from that vulnerable, 'unsafe' place of your heart, you have cheaply traded your birthright and will find it impossible to live in the abundance of God's love.

Whenever the mind sees itself in jeopardy, it devises a clever new strategy as part of its game. The very thing that has the potential to place you into the expansiveness of the heart — the presence of love — is what the mind will seek to encapsulate in a box (or better, eliminate) as fast as possible.

Uncertainty about my influence among the elders of the Jewish people, who were not prepared to change their way of life and thinking, allowed them to sow seeds of fear with lies and deceit. In exercising their authority, they easily misled the people by calling my Father's miracles the work of the devil.

As the people's focus shifted from the expansiveness of the heart to the misgivings of the mind, the elders tricked them into a box that kept them separate from the very love that had healed them.

Once again, men believed in the destructive words of ignorant minds that professed to know God and His will. The Sanhedrin and the Pharisees perceived me as a threat to their way of life.

To stay in control of their hard-earned power within the Temple, they had to deny the fulfillment of Biblical prophesies and scorn the suggestion that I was the messiah sent by God.

They were men who had spent their lives studying scripture and making their way to the top of the religious establishment. The missing link between their work and their calling was the experience of God's love.

These were good men, but the mind could not acknowledge what the heart did not feel. There was nothing else they could do other than have me killed.

They, too, had a cloud around the heart, and the truth was tucked away in the bottom of the largest and strongest box of all. This is the box that allows those with authority and influence within their religious structures to commit unthinkable crimes in the name of God.

My Father and I weep when those called to His service pridefully ignore their hearts and speak to our beloved children with hurtful words and act out pain-filled deeds.

Perhaps now you can better understand how the people of two thousand years ago were so easily led, mob-like, into clamoring for the release of Barabbas. A thief and a bully they could understand and relate to.

He represented normalcy. Even though many had been on the wrong end of the stick where Barabbas was concerned, he only acted in congruence with their mindset and culture.

On the other hand, my life demonstrated that greed and judgment were unacceptable and that forgiveness was essential for personal and societal balance.

I reminded people of the life from which they had strayed.

They were not happy, no more than you have been happy, to give up the way of life they had come to know, accept and ultimately prefer.

I understand this is a choice made from fear.
To change will mean a whole new world. The fears you have assimilated dictate the choice of staying in the world you know rather than moving into the one you do not know.

Once you decide you will no longer play this game and that you want to break free of the boxes of your beliefs, the first thing to do is say "No" to the fears of your mind. Accept they exist and make the decision to walk into the heart anyway, reconnecting with the guidance and wisdom of God which is always available to you there.

That guidance and wisdom lives within you.
You do not have to go to another person to connect with God. Another person can only help to remind you of this truth.

God lives within your heart and the heart of every cell of your being.

You are connected to the source of love by the source of love.

My brother Buddha explained this subject with a simple metaphor.

One of Buddha's disciples asked for help to understand how he could be a part of the oneness of all life when he felt so separate from everyone and everything. Buddha took out a handkerchief and said, "Look, I will tie six knots into this handkerchief. They are all individual knots but they still belong to the one handkerchief. They are all different from each other yet still remain part of the whole of the fabric."

Your individuality is not separation from God or your fellow human beings. It is a celebration of the vastness of God's creativity. This creativity lives within you.

Have you been moved to tears when experiencing heart-inspired music, art and design? Has the sunset ever 'taken your breath away' with its magnificence?

You are interacting not only with your physical senses of sight and hearing but also with your non-physical sense of intuition. You are exercising the very creativity that makes humans so extraordinary.

You know who you are. You know where you have come from. Nature, beauty and the wonder of your world are constant reminders.

Because the mind cannot completely dilute the impact of nature, the magic of your creativity, or the wonder of God's angels and emissaries, it has been forced to confront its limitations. This makes it afraid.

The mind has dulled your senses and limited your memory out of its own fear of redundancy and demotion. In deceiving you, the mind has deceived itself into believing it could actually become unimportant if the heart were to have its say. The mind has forgotten the significance of its original role.

You are not oblivious to the wonders of the world.
You constantly sense and experience evidence of God all around you.

The heart and the awareness associated with it — which processes all information coming at you from all directions — needs the mind to develop consciousness.

Consciousness is developed throughout your life and, indeed, throughout your multiple lifetimes.
It is not foundational like the heart and heart's awareness.

As you allow the heart to guide the mind into God consciousness, you increasingly experience the fullness of a human life as God intended it to be.

Without the heart's guidance and awareness, you are a human doing, not a human being.

All the games of the mind have you 'doing' so many things, filling your minds and lives with so much busy-ness that you have no time or space for yourself or each other.

Taking yourself to higher and higher levels of love means making new choices in your life and changing how you do things. This new awareness guides you to seek the answers to your most important questions from a wise and timeless source.

That source is the wisdom and love of God residing within you, deep within your heart.

To verify that it is God's word, remember this: if the

information fills you with joy and wonder with its expansive, magnanimous truth, you know it is the heart speaking.

If the information stimulates fear, negativity or pain, you know your mind has hooked you back into a game.
When the answers to your questions call you to inflict unnecessary pain in any form on any living being, you can be sure that it is not God's word.

Be aware of your mind trying to tell you how difficult and useless these words are, for I can already hear it trying to talk to you.

"Hang on! Just think, this could mean I would have to change the way I live. Once I am in my heart I will no longer be able to indulge myself as a sexual predator; judging others will be out; lying to save myself will no longer be acceptable. I will have to be faithful to my partner and the excesses of alcohol and the abuse of my body will have to cease. It will hurt me to hurt others and I will no longer be able to scare myself with wild and fantastic imaginings." The list goes on.

Do not deceive yourself into thinking that living in balance as a divine child of God means boredom.
Balance does not mean boredom.

On the contrary, those who live through the heart whilst walking your world in human form have the least boring lives of anyone.

Once you choose to cease this madness that runs your lives,

you will know every soul as a brother or sister, a son or daughter, a mother or father. Your desire for love will not manifest as sexual deviation, perversion, or excess.

The false perception that sex is a way of having love and alleviating loneliness is far from the truth. This is the mind's rationalization — another game — that brings pain, unfulfillment and greater disappointment.

Sexuality as intended by God is a divine expression of love between a man and a woman whose hearts have opened and committed to each other.

To touch another is a sacred honor.
To open your entire being on every dimension, including sexual, is the most complete and intimate sharing of love. In this ultimate expression of love with your beloved, the heart feels the oneness and union of love with God and the beloved simultaneously.

It is easy to see how the mind scored triumphantly in the sexual game it invented. Take the heart out of the equation and sexual intimacy becomes something to separate one heart from the other, setting yet another destructive game into play.

This would have to be one of the most soul-destroying and heartbreaking games of them all and one of the most effective at maintaining and reinforcing separation.

Truly, the love you seek is found within you.
Deep inside your heart and safe forever is the love,
acceptance and understanding you have been searching for.

No other person can satisfy your longing for love or need
for acceptance. In remembering who you are you discover
how worthy you are of your own love and acceptance.

Once you begin to live through the heart, you will discover
sharing love more rewarding than anything else.
I am not speaking only about sexuality here.

The love expressed within families and between partners,
neighbors and the people you meet each day will satisfy
your heart and fill it with peace and joy.

**No matter what else you believe, nor what other fears
you still cling to, when you express the love that you are
without fear you will always find happiness in your life.**

You will experience the reality of God because it is God
who generates this love and happiness. Nothing other than
love can generate this experience.

Every being wants love, acceptance and abundance in their
lives. The way to achieve a happy, healthy and fulfilling life
is to be what you want to experience.

If you want love in your life, then be love.
If you desire nurturing, acceptance and support, learn to
nurture, accept and support others.

When you know you are worthy of living in God's
abundance, you will generously give of yourself, of your
time, energy, and creativity.
As you give, so shall you receive.

Graciously give from your heart; do not begrudge or give with the expectation of return. Stay alert to the tricks of the mind. If your motives are to gain recognition and fame, the giving has a different energy.

Any form of manipulation cuts the energetic link of love to and from the heart.

You might feel smart and self-satisfied after manipulating situations and people to get what you want, but this is self-deception. People will no longer trust you when they realize how you have treated them.

Spirit is expansive. Its very nature is generous. The easiest way to sabotage the expansiveness of your heart is to create separation by manipulative thoughts.

Feelings arise from the heart, the centre of your being where the seed of God resides. It is the focal point of your communication with God. If allowed, the mind seizes the opportunity to distort these feelings in order to serve its own agenda.

For instance, your mind may want you to be recognized for your heart-inspired acts of goodness and charity. Your heart, the source of the inspiration, has no need or desire for recognition. The mind, on the other hand, desperately seeks acceptance.

When you deny the promptings of the heart and choose to follow the thoughts of your mind, it is likely to result in confusion, delusion or denial.

Fear of doing and saying the wrong thing may creep in.
Fear of making the wrong moves may appear in the games you pretend to not even know you are playing.
Sooner or later negativity, confusion and pain result from playing the game.

The only being the heart wishes to please is God.

As an integral part of the One Spirit, your heart knows everything you do and say is known by God.
This simplicity and beauty cannot come from anywhere other than the heart.

The essential prerequisite for wholeness and thus fulfillment is to maintain awareness of the heart, know the truth, and live with the innocence of a child.

God has no desire to keep you small and ignorant of who you are. If He made your choices, you would not be living in pain. You would not be confined in the boxes built over thousands of years of accumulated corruption from your original state.

It is time to stop playing this game of ignorance.
Ignorance is not bliss. Be brave.
Know all the help you need is available to you.

I am here, living within your heart.
The angelic realm, along with all the other dimensions of God's creation, is here to love and support you back into wholeness.

If you want to experience wholeness, you must live truth.

TRUTH, LIES AND **LOVE**

That means your quest to discover what the truth is for you must be your ongoing priority.

What untruth have you told yourself that you need to change?

Many pretend to know a lot. For instance, they may speak with eloquence and great learning of theology and God, yet so often the information is not the truth. Religious institutions were created to be places where people could gather and share in the dynamic of God's words and His love.

When you believe anyone who tells you that the only way to know God is through a particular church, institution or theology, you have played into the hands of separation.

Separation, which encompasses judgment and fragmentation, is the opposite of wholeness.

Wholeness comes when you are free to live in your heart and to love so fully that telling the truth is no longer frightening and living the truth is the only choice.

How easy is it to trick yourself into believing you are speaking the truth when you are not?
How many times have you done it?
How many times have you given yourself the perfect excuse for doing so?

This is denial of reality. It is simply a case of rationalizing and justifying lying. You know in your heart when you are not telling the truth. Perhaps there is a moment of discomfort, but once you have justified separating reality into lies with your own unique brand of fantasy, you are content playing the game just as you always have.

The sad thing is, everyone knows through their connection to the multi-dimensionality of life what is happening, yet most allow the lies to continue and the games to go on.

Every living being is connected to every other living being. Through this energetic connection information may be transferred from one being to another, from God, from angels and from any person whether in physical form or not.

The social set-up and belief system that you have allowed to govern your life separates you from this knowledge and allows you to deceive each other by dulling your senses to this connection.

Ignorance and deception notwithstanding, you have never been separated from God, your heart, or this information. Exercise your right to ask for direct guidance and inspiration. Do not give away that responsibility to others you suppose are more qualified than you to seek advice from God.

There is no one more qualified to ask God about your life than you. You can always access the truth when you ask honestly through the heart — your most direct connection to God.

The truth is, you are incredibly wise and have a direct link to your Creator. This direct link resides within your heart and yet you insist on playing dumb and pretending you are separate. Does this suit your purpose? How would you get enjoyment out of your games if you took responsibility for your life?

There would be no fun at all if you could not blame your parents, siblings, friends or whoever else is handy.
Blame separates you from these people and cements the unhappiness. But the mind is happy, because you are right and they are wrong. And, they of course, are to blame and responsible for causing your decisions.

Life happens. Events occur.
They give us the opportunity to choose to go into our hearts, to see the big picture and grow from every pain-filled experience.

If you were no longer attached to the games you have created, you would confront the truth of why you and the world are in these situations. You would expand your mind by allowing the heart to address your problems.

At the core of all problems is humanity's reluctance to accept and live the oneness of all life. The interwoven tapestry of creation has not singled you out and cast you aside to fend for yourself. God has not separated Himself from you nor from any of the people of this world.

You have separated yourselves from Him.

I repeated my simple message so many different ways, demonstrating the love, acceptance and inclusion of all through God's love.

JESUS WEEPS

I kept reminding my disciples that God does not exclude anyone from His love.

The parable about the lost sheep, where the shepherd left the flock to find the one that had strayed from the herd, emphasized that not one soul is unimportant to God.

Every day, in every way, it was my job to demonstrate God's love and acceptance by accepting all people into my life, regardless of their gender, religious upbringing, color or nationality.

God's words do not belong exclusively to any man or woman, race, color, or creed. Who is more important to God than another? Who will be the judge of that? Not I.

My disciples gave up the lives they had been living because God touched that seed of Christ consciousness within them at the same time I appeared before them.
Their hearts soared from that expanded place.

I spent many hours leading them back into the heart — that place they were in when they accepted the challenge to leave their everyday lives and join me.

The heart longs to regain its God-given role.
A part of you will always remember who you are and the exhilarating experience of living from within God's love.

The expanded hearts of my disciples and those who loved me allowed their hearts to make the decision to give up the mundane world of the mind and to journey into their hearts, where they could once again connect with the fullness of their souls.

From this place their choices were clear.
From this place, the wisdom of the heart helped the mind to choose God.

However, the games of the mind had long since become ingrained into the memory of their being. They had to remain aware of the mind's machinations in order to stay balanced.

With so many new and powerful experiences happening daily, it was an ongoing challenge for them to keep the mind from putting my words into a box so they could play their former games.

They wanted to differentiate the Jews from the Gentiles, the men from the women, themselves from each other.

I understood this corruption of the truth.
It was the reason for my life.
These men and women who traveled with me were the gauge I used to see if I was being understood.

As they acted out their confusion and allowed their minds to justify separation and judgment, I changed the stories but continued to give the same message.

Each story touched a layer of the heart but in different ways, depending on each individual's stage in his or her life. Those suffering the most were willing to hear my words from their heart.

After so many lifetimes of denial, it almost always takes traumatic pain to motivate one to pay the price of change. The good news is that the price is simply knowing — then living — the truth.

Many were eager to believe there could be more to life than what they had experienced. But such great suffering had touched the heart that only the very brave were prepared to be vulnerable and to love.

I say this because the more grief the heart has known, the more the mind insulates it. Dulling and numbing one's true feelings is the way of denial; it is the way to separate the heart from the head.

The misuse and abuse of sex, alcohol, food, caffeine, tobacco and various other mind-changing drugs are tactics of the mind. However, when the effects — numbing or euphoric or whatever — wear off, reality hits home harder than ever.

The body now has to cope with the health consequences of these substances, as well as the emotional havoc and real-life problems these choices wreak in one's life.

God has designed your amazing body to self-regulate, to heal and regenerate. The brain releases into the nervous system the necessary chemicals and electrical impulses that impel any needed responses in all parts of the body.

When you feel fear and choose the path that perpetuates your destructive games, the chemicals released trigger harmful responses.

TRUTH, LIES AND **LOVE**

This is the body's way of communicating that there is something wrong with the way you are thinking.

As masters of separation, you have come to regard yourself primarily as your mind and have denied the intelligence of the body, the awareness of your heart and the existence of your soul.

In doing this you react to the pain and deal only with the symptoms, as though your body has turned against you for no reason at all.

Of course there are those who regard disease, pain and suffering as punishment from God for doing wrong.
This implies that God intends to instill fear into His children for listening to each others' lies, for participating in the greed of this world, and for creating hell on Earth where once was heaven.

For as long as you need to hear it, I will continue to tell you that to blame God for any of the ills of this world today is just another game, an easy way out.

It's very much like blaming your parents for your unhappiness when you need to accept responsibility for your decisions. Only then can you learn wisdom from every circumstance and situation.

You always have a choice about what you think.
You can choose to allow your hearts to choose right action or you can allow the mind to choose a course that perpetuates games, which leads to pain and death.

This is so because you are powerful beyond your wildest
dreams. As powerfully as you can love and create beauty
so, too, you can create chaos and destruction.

It always comes down to the choices you are prepared
to make at any given moment.

Your body does not miss a thing. It listens via every cell to
your choices and reacts accordingly. It will not lie to you.
It is not in denial of the pain in your life. It alerts you to
the consequences of false thinking and wrong action.

You are an expression of God's love.
The body is your vehicle of expression in physical life and
it has never forgotten its origin and Creator.
The body is spiritually intelligent.

The body's commitment to truth and its need to live in harmony with its Creator can be in such great conflict with your games that illness results and survival can even become impossible.

Thus, when you only treat the symptoms of disease (which is
the body being ill at ease with your fears and the decisions
made from those fears) it may die rather than heal.

God did not make these choices for you.
The truth is, you caused the body's cry for help by your
decisions, judgments and your willingness to choose wrong
action.

Whatever the fear, whatever the problem, the body
eventually brings you to a place of acknowledgment.

For instance, if a woman does not believe she deserves a loving relationship, if she continually judges others as more beautiful, more talented, more worthy, her love relationships will reflect these thoughts.

Her partners will look at and see other women as sexually desirable. Their infidelity and her feelings of betrayal will eat away at the very core of her womanhood.

The woman who believes she is not worthy of love gives this devastating script to her partners. At first, they will be perplexed that this beautiful woman expects to be betrayed and let down. However, it does not take people long to get the hang of each others' games.

With the expertise of award-winning actors, her partners will read her script and begin to lie and cheat on her.

Her body, in its wisdom, will not allow the game to continue. However, its only way to be heard is to create pain. The body is crying out for her to question her life. To change her script and to see herself as God sees her.

In a case like this, her female organs might well feel as if they are being eaten away. Cancer of the breasts, ovaries, cervix and/or the womb is a likely result.
God created you as spiritually intelligent beings.
Your body has never forgotten this.

By accepting responsibility for the judgments and decisions of your past, you will see that your life is a culmination of all the choices you have ever made.

JESUS WEEPS

Every choice that separates you from the love that is
your heart separates you from God.

Remember, your true essence is love.
Love is who you are. Every soul, including you, lives with
the light of God within them.

It is your choice to live the light that you are or to hide
that light so that eventually not even you can find it.
Over numerous lifetimes, the denial of love has diminished
the light of God.

Abundance is integral to love's nature.
Without love the fear of scarcity grabs your heart and
squeezes it shut.

The mind then takes over from the pain-filled heart and the
seeds of greed are sown in the fertile ground of fear.

Need (insufficiency) mixed with fear is the most
devastating of man's illusions for it produces greed.
Greed turns brother against brother, race against race
and nation against nation.

With greed, justice goes out the door, for a fearful mind
will convince you that you are doing the right thing by
stealing from another, for killing to get what you want
because you think you need it. That the end justifies the
means.

Without justice there is no balance.
Justice is the principle of balance in action.
Buddha expressed this perfectly when he explained the

necessity of taking the middle path as we walked through our lives.

Love is the fulcrum of a balanced heart.
The loving heart knows that love is a magnet to more love and that balance is the way to put a stop to greed.

Love gives of itself without expectation of anything in return. A life without love will be full of disappointments and pain, as your expectations will rarely be fulfilled.

When the choices and actions of the fear-filled mind enshroud the heart, its power to attract love diminishes. You then lose your power to choose freedom and experience joy.

The brave heart uses its wisdom to come into balance and wholeness, to find the truth and know God once more.

My life opened avenues of trust and inspiration for those ready to take the plunge back into wholeness and truth.

When you live from within the wholeness of God's heart, there is no such thing as suffering; there is no confusion, only clarity; no imperfection, only purity.
God is purity, truth, honesty, beauty.

God is not responsible for our lies, illusions, games or pain. As a race, humanity has mastered that without any help from Him whatsoever.

Do you really think God wants you to suffer?

JESUS WEEPS

If and when you suffer, God suffers with you.
When you know joy, God rejoices.

My mission was to help you remember God; to remember
the most important thing in the world.

**You are a divine child of God. God lives inside you.
Your heart is the center of His existence within you and
His desire is for you to be happy.**

**Your Creator wants you to enjoy your life as a human
being — to have as much fun as you can have in a body —
from a place of wholeness and truth.**

The truth is you have never been separated from God.
This is impossible.

And yet, most people feel disconnected from each other
and from God.

There is a monkey on your back.
This monkey is not a part of your soul or your body.
Yet, it is so familiar, it seems attached to you.

It whispers in your ear, frightening your heart with lies and
shrouding the light that you are with the illusion of fear
and separation.

You also have an angel with you.
You can hear the guidance, love and support of this angel
when you listen with your heart.

You have listened to the misguidance and destructive lies of the monkey for so long that your innate ability to choose right from wrong has been greatly reduced.

With a growing awareness of yourself as a spiritual being comes increasing hunger to know the truth about yourself. But, the veil of forgetfulness and the cumulative impact of deception and denial has disempowered you and placed your love in jeopardy.

That which you love is what drives you; you will always strive towards that which makes you happy.
So, whatever you are happiest experiencing within your life is what you will do and where you will be.

Most believe you can have only what you think you deserve and no more. And so, you reach for what you love within the boxes you have created for yourself.

These boxes stifle your heart.
The true love of your heart is replaced by things the mind loves — drugs, abuse of alcohol, food or sex, even killing for your country and for God.

God does not interfere with your choices.
But, God rejoices when you take up your right of free will and live from the love of your heart, choosing truth over lies, wholeness over self-pity, chaos, pain and suffering.

You are being called forth as of this moment to be wise, to embark on a journey of discovery. And, no matter how painful the truths revealed to you may be, to persevere.

JESUS WEEPS

Say "no" to the boxes and structures of your world before they destroy you (and your world) as they crucified me. Utilize your direct link with God once again and insist your heart reclaim its power over your mind.

This means you must allow yourself to consciously feel your feelings.

Feelings, especially love, have been squashed for so long. Love has almost become a cliché.
Knowing God is not a function of the mind; rather, it requires honest acceptance of your true feelings.

It is not weakness to love, nurture and support yourself and others.

**In fact, to be vulnerable to your heart right now is the single most brave and powerful thing you can do.
It will enable you to be free to heal.**

All healing is accomplished through love.
No one has ever healed through hatred. But, many have died through hatred, both their own hatred and the hatred of others.

Once you accept your right to live without the interference of the judgments of others and to participate in the wonder of living from within God's heart, you will become whole.

You will be healed. The torn fissures of your heart will fill with the light of God and you will know the truth of these words. Your whole being will expand, and the love within your heart will answer your deepest questions.

The truth has been hidden for so long and you have deceived yourself so often that sometimes the answers will surprise you. But the answers will also bring joy to your heart.

Happiness and joy is your natural state of being.

You have lived so many lifetimes from your mind instead of from your heart that this is hard to believe, I know.

When you share ideas and philosophies about love and God, it is only the mind talking if you have not experienced that love and if you do not have a genuine relationship with God.

For most people at this time, nothing is harder than to know when they are experiencing something in their heart rather than saying something they merely think is the truth.

Without the fullness of the experience, including feeling and emotion, how can you know what you are talking about?
This is the challenge of knowing God.

Without remembering God or experiencing God, how do you bring yourself back to knowing God? Thus, for most people now, my Father is a mere concept, an idea, an abstraction.

I want you to go beyond ideas.
Jump out of the boxes that have you afraid to live in your heart and you will expand your life a thousand-fold.

You ask yourself if love is an emotion, something to control. You cannot control love. It is not an emotion or an action. Love simply is!

Love is a wondrous mystery. It does not fit into any boxes man's mind can devise. Love can be experienced as a feeling that permeates your entire being. You can have glimpses of love when you open yourselves up to the wisdom of your heart, to compassion and forgiveness.

Once you begin to understand the love God has for you, you know you are held in the arms of your adoring Father and, no matter how big you grow, He never lets you go.

Then you remember what has been missing and how life could be. Excited, you begin to talk about love because you have had a moment experiencing it, a moment expressing it, a moment feeling it.

However, the mind can still create ways to block your experience of God's love, stunting the growth of your awareness of it.

The mind has crowded God out.
Using fear, the ultimate obstacle to wholeness, it tells you it is not safe to love. Once again, you separate yourself from who you really are.

Separation means you no longer live with the memory of God growing within you. You inhibit your awareness of God as you separate yourself — when you refuse to love, when you refuse to accept that there is an order to all things and that you do not have to control it.

Success in life is assured by understanding who you are.
If you do the right thing by God, you do right by yourself and therefore the right thing by everyone else in your life.

TRUTH, LIES AND **LOVE**

Doing the right thing means telling the truth, living the truth, not entertaining yourself with the games that you play, and refusing to accept unacceptable behavior from yourself or others.

Remember, God does not judge you. Do not judge one another. It is your privilege and purpose to know God more fully in this lifetime than any other lifetime since you were an Earth angel. What an honor it is; what a great soul you are. Start living your greatness.

Truly, you should be in awe of yourself, of the greatness of who you are, and of God. Know that God is in awe of you, awesome one! What more do you need to know?
When you live wholeness and truth, you live from the greatness of who you are. You will not play mankind's destructive games any longer, nor will you teach your sons and daughters these games.

As you demonstrate that wholeness is possible, you will sow seeds for the transformation of this world.

What could stop you from stepping into wholeness?
Only the unwillingness to move through the fears of loving fully and moving into truth.

**Fears have power only if you believe them.
The awakened heart has no fear.
Bravely arouse your heart. Enter it.
And you will have no fear.**

Are you willing to discover why you do what you do and change it in order to know God?

God will never reject you. As you become more truthful, loving and vulnerable you will just live deeper within God's heart; you will be safe.

Be childlike. Be honest. You can tell your Father that you do not want Him to go away ever again; that you want your Father, your Creator, your Lord and God to stay with you forever.

In truth there is nowhere else that He can be — it is only you who goes away, not God.

You are being pushed by the wisdom of your own unique soul to be more now — not tomorrow, not next year — now! Humanity's limited spiritual I.Q. soars as you move into the era of the heart.

Command your mind to come into balance.
Listen to the wisdom and knowledge of your heart and act on it. Only in this way can you reclaim your birthright.

Be diligent. You will discover the tricks of the mind when you listen to your thoughts with objectivity. Be alert. Reject anything your mind tells you that denies love, forgiveness, compassion, reconciliation and harmony.

Your soul knows you have nothing to fear when you live from the heart. The heart's decisions are from that expanded place that always deals with the truth, that sees the big picture and that alone has the divine capability of identifying the highest good for all concerned.
The whole, fully-functioning heart will tell you if you are on the right track or not.

Ask and you shall receive the loving guidance of our Father.
And I will be there in your heart. For who am I?
I am that part of you speaking to you now.
I am the wisdom of the One Spirit that lives within you.
Not outside of you, not separate from you.

Invite your heart to listen as you read these words.
These words are from your own heart.
They have not come from outside of who you are.
You are listening to yourself speaking to your self.
The soul of your being is guiding you.

Every living soul has access at all times to its Creator.
It can be no other way.

Scientists delving into quantum physics and scholars researching the way the world works have already confirmed the oneness of all life.

God lives within everything and everyone.
This does not mean God chooses your responses or is accountable for the actions of all life.

Your parents brought your physical being into this world but they are not the decision-makers of your whole life.

There comes a time when their influence over you diminishes and, suddenly, you know so much more than they know. (How old were you when you stopped listening to your parents?)

Lack of respect and presumptuous, all-knowing self-confidence are manifesting at younger and younger ages.

The lucky ones outgrow this stage and begin to seek
guidance, wisdom and truth from those who love them
and have learned through experience.

This is analogous to your relationship with God.
You have presumed for too long to know more than your
Father, and you have made up stories with no substance
to fool yourselves and others.

Well, you are not a baby any more and it is time to face
facts. In terms of the evolution of your soul, you are hardly
a teenager either!

**You have come to that amazing point in the progression
of your soul when wisdom is knocking on your door.
The stage is set for you to take the biggest leap forward
in the evolution of consciousness since the devolution
from Earth angel to human.**

Open the door.

Reassure your heart that it is safe to love again.
Command your mind to stop feeding the heart's fears and
diligently live the truth.

Many people have opened this evolutionary door and
stepped through into a new and magical future.

These brave ones and many of the children being born
at an increasing rate in the last two decades are beginning
to experience the multi-dimensionality of spiritually
intelligent beings. They know when you are playing a game
and will call you forth to know and tell the truth.

It is time to choose. You can hold on to the old way of living and the old values that allowed you to continue to live in ignorance of the real truth. Or, you can choose the bliss of freedom from the insidious games that keep hearts numb and minds in turmoil.

When you stop focusing on everything external in your life, you will begin to hear the answers and guidance you sought from others coming from the well-spring of wisdom that resides within you.

Do you see first and then believe?
Or do you believe, and then see?

Trust the truth of my words.
Then you will develop your intuition and your recognition of a higher order, of more and different vibrations than what you are aware of today.

Love is the catalyst that expands your being.

The wisdom of your heart is the key to this evolution back into the multi-dimensional totality of the world in which you live.

Love is the matrix from which you were created.
Love is the essence of who you are.
Aligning yourself back into a fearless heart is realigning yourself with more of who you really are...which is one with God.

I understand that even reading these words may throw your heart into fear.

But no matter how fearful your heart and how well the mind uses this fear to keep you from evolving, you cannot stop the truth from emerging.

Whether it is in this lifetime or the next or the next, you will eventually remember who you are, which is who you have always been.

The very reason I walked among you was to remind you that you are so much more than your bodies, minds and physical senses. You are the love of the Creator in human form.

Humanity has become spiritually over-simplistic and denied the multi-dimensionality of all life.

We wept as we watched from the sidelines where you kept us, as you separated, judged and excluded us from your lives. But that does not mean we did not exist.

Not only do we exist, but at this critical moment of choice we continue to assist you in any way we can.

The focus of my life was not about my death on a cross. It was about being a bright shining star, a guiding light in the midst of so much darkness.

Every angelic being and every one of my brothers and sisters who come to you through God's grace to help and be of guidance acts as a light in the darkness of ignorance and pain.

We come to communicate with your heart on behalf of your soul, to urge you to look more carefully at what you believe to be the truth. The big picture (and God's plan) does not include fears that create fantasies and illusions that keep you ignorant of who you really are.

When you believe this message, you will live the truth and become whole. This means rewriting your personal script to live life with joy, peace and the innocence of a heart having fun.

Humanity's script must change. Its survival requires it. As one changes, so, like a stone dropped into a pond, will the ripples go out and affect many others. The more changes for the better you make in your life, the more you also will become a bright shining star in the darkness.

Each time you confront and disempower one of your fears, you lighten the load of the heart and help it learn to trust itself again.

Be discerning.
Seize this opportunity to move through the fears that bog you down and prevent you from knowing God.

Your heart will learn to trust God again.

The heart's greatest desire is to know God in every beat.

Unburden your mind. Like a loving parent, reassure your mind with firm, consistent guidance. You can do it!

JESUS WEEPS

Unshackle your heart; give it permission to speak freely to you without fear. Make its free and fearless communication with you your highest priority.

My wisdom and all that I am will always be a part of you. All that I am will remain with you, loving and supporting you.

I am listening.
I am with you always.
I love you.